Clippings from
Orene's Garden:

A Southern Gardener's Year

Orene Horton

To Peggy –

Happy gardening!

Mar. 1, 2005   *Tete Horton*

CORINTHIAN
BOOKS

Mount Pleasant, S. C.

Publishers Cataloging-in-Publication Data

(Provided by Quality Books, Inc.)

Horton, Orene.
    Clippings from Orene's Garden : A Southern gardener's
    year / Orene Horton. -- 1st ed.
    p. cm.
    Includes bibilographical references and index.
    LCCN 2002117085
    ISBN 1929175353

    1. Gardening--Southern States. I. Title.

SB453.2.S66H67 2003   635'.0975
                                          QBI03-200022

First Edition:

    First printing, March 2003

This book is printed on archival-quality paper that meets the guidelines for
performance and durability of the Committee on Production Guidelines for Book
Longevity for the Council on Library Resources.

Versions of these articles appeared as Orene Horton's gardening
columns in *The State,* or as articles in *Columbia Metropolitan* magazine.

Corinthian Books
P. O. Box 1898
Mt. Pleasant, SC 29465-1898

http://www.corinthianbooks.com

In Memoriam

Orene Stroud Horton
1944 – 2002

"A garden is ageless and the gardener becomes ageless too,
as ageless as the wind, the rain, the sun, summer and winter,
for he becomes one with them all."

Hanna Rion

Contents

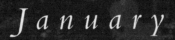

January

One Gardener's Resolutions

All things seem possible in January. Sipping a cup of tea in my easy chair before a crackling fire, with a basket of newly arrived gardening catalogs beside me, I can conquer the world. Visions of Wordsworthian fields of daffodils for spring and Gertrude-Jekyll-style borders for summer with colors that melt into perfect harmony — these can surely be mine. This is the time to make my new year's gardening resolutions. By June, I will have tempered my expectations, though not abandoned them. Feel free to adopt any resolutions that fit your needs or ambitions.

I resolve to write in my garden diary every week and to photograph great garden successes, as well as failures. I usually have slide film in my camera, but a snapshot is something that can be put in a notebook and referred to easily later.

I resolve to order early — roses, bulbs, choice shrubs, and perennials. It's amazing how fast winter melts into spring.

I resolve to read more of my garden magazines. I always thumb through them when they come, but it's hard to get back to read all of them. This is a very good way to increase my gardening knowledge.

I resolve to put out beer as slug bait at the first sign of attack and to keep it replenished. Surely I can outsmart a lowly slug, a creature so far beneath me on the food chain. I have found that beer can be diluted by half and still be effective. I buy the cheapest brand and try to look nonchalant as the grocery store cashier rings up my purchase.

In the front yard, I can put the beer in open jar lids sunk into the ground. However, in the backyard, we have two dachshunds with beer-loving genes. There I fill plastic margarine tubs, having cut into the lids a hole large enough for a slug's body but too small for a dog's tongue.

I resolve to write all fertilization, pruning, and spraying schedules on my Master Gardener Calendar. I want to keep roses and annuals blooming by remembering to fertilize pansies with a liquid fertilizer every two weeks during their growing seasons and roses once a month. Bulbs need to be fertilized with a special bulb fertilizer when the foliage is just coming up. Beds must be top-dressed with compost in the spring and again in the fall.

I resolve to plan before I buy plants. I will walk around the garden and see what needs to be replaced. Listing all the pots and beds where new plants will be needed, I will try to plan my color combinations and make a list to take with me to the nursery. I will decide early in the year which plants I can grow from seed and order them, but try to resist the temptation to order more than I can use.

I resolve to always write down where I have planted things. Labels have the worst tendency to disappear. I honestly think squirrels move them to other places and delight in my confusion. A picture of the bed in bloom would help identify plants. A rough sketch of the bed with the approximate location of where something was planted is helpful, or just a written description of where I put those autumn-flowering crocuses. Giving a name to each of my beds helps me to know that there are miniature daffodils under the dogwood tree in the front bed along the driveway.

I resolve to walk around my garden every day, even in the winter, lest I miss the blooms of the tiny winter-blooming Algerian iris (*Iris unguicularis*). Aphid infestations will be much easier to treat with just a spray of liquid insecticidal soap if they are caught early enough.

I resolve not to let a rampant ground cover, such as variegated *Vinca major*, get ahead of me. Pretty as it is, it will soon take over a bed if not faithfully rooted out. It makes a great trailing plant for large containers but only for those that are located on a hard surface, not the ground. Once it touches the ground, it sprouts roots and gallops off to climb into shrubs and choke out little crocuses or strawberry begonias and any other small treasure in its path.

I resolve to write down all my resolutions so that I can look back next January and get a good chuckle. Perhaps I can live up to some of them, but others can just be moved onto next year's list.

Finally, I resolve to enjoy my garden more. I want to take time out from gardening work and actually sit on my garden bench, even though this will mean squelching my tendency to see something that needs to be done everywhere I look. I want to enjoy what I've done already. I want to smell my roses and watch a moonflower unfurl at dusk. And I want to drink more lemonade.

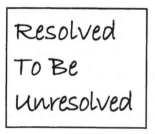

It's resolution time again. We gardeners, having only the very best of intentions, do hereby promise this year to _____ (you fill in the blank). Two years ago, I fearlessly wrote about my resolutions for the new year. I thought it might be telling to revisit that list and see how I fared.

Sadly, I learned that I am not as resolute as I imagined. I still haven't developed the habit of writing in my garden journal every week, and I don't order everything early. I also haven't walked around the garden every day to look for problems. Insects surely cannot eat that fast. So, instead, I walk around several times a week. I do take care of problems as soon as I discover them. But measures like putting saucers of beer out to catch slugs do get to be a chore after a month or so.

The ability to keep meticulous records of fertilization, pruning, and spraying schedules has eluded me. But I have been faithful about feeding my bulbs with bulb fertilizer when they start to come up and again after they finish blooming. Anyone who has bought and planted hundreds of bulbs has too much invested in money and muscle not to take good care of them.

Keeping my compost pile going has been easy. You have to put those mushy vegetables from the back of the refrigerator and all those rinds and peelings somewhere. And it's no more trouble to rake leaves into the compost pile than into the street. The hard part is making sure to use that compost (this requires heavy lifting) on my beds every spring and fall.

I have failed miserably to always plan before I buy plants. Even though I usually go to the garden center with a list of the areas where I need plants, I always get sidetracked when I see other interesting and desirable ones. Much to the plant vendors' delight, I am easily tempted to buy things that I have no earthly idea where to plant. But it's like falling in love. We lose our sense of perspective.

Naming all my different planting areas was easy, and it is a great help when I'm making lists of things to do and to plant in my garden. Unwanted creeping plants, such as variegated vinca, still pop up in beds where I didn't get them all rogued out. If I don't remain diligent in pulling them out right away, they will regain a foothold.

My final resolution was to enjoy my garden more, to smell the roses, to sit on the bench and drink more lemonade. And I do find this one easier to keep than some others. I never tire of seeing the flowers of a star magnolia unfurl, and my nose can never get enough of fragrant plants like winter honeysuckle, winter daphne, witch hazel, and Japanese flowering apricot.

I enjoy sharing my garden with other people, especially when it's looking its best.

So, what can I resolve this year? Not to resolve anything? Maybe just to learn more about the plants I grow; to keep rearranging beds that I know I'll never get right; to keep rushing inside for my camera to capture a vignette of color and form at the perfect moment; and to collect seeds from my plants after they bloom so I can participate in seed exchanges.

I will also try to share my experiences with others so they won't make some of my mistakes and may experience some of my successes. Happy New Gardening Year!

Seeds Hold Magical Promise

There's something magical about seeds. Pour out a packet of flower or vegetable seeds into your hand and think of the promise they hold. Given time, the right soil, light, water, temperature, and care, these seeds will produce flowers to charm you or vegetables to feed you.

I must admit that I am a bit late in starting my seeds this year. Maybe it's because I couldn't make up my mind which to choose among the myriad compelling choices available in my stack of seed catalogs. I usually start most of my seeds in January or February. Don't think you have to have a greenhouse to grow them. Although I've longed for one for years, lack of space forces me to make do with my less-than-ideal situation. I manage to produce enough successes to keep me trying.

My setup includes an old door resting on brick legs in the basement. Two sets of adjustable shop lights hang over the table. I try to keep the fluorescent tubes about two to four feet from the sprouting seeds. For containers, I use anything that will hold soil and can have drainage holes punched in the bottom, mostly styrofoam or plastic containers from the grocery store. Strawberry or mushroom containers make ideal mini-greenhouses because they come with a transparent lid to hold in humidity. Without a mist system like the commercial growers have, you have to create your own climate control. Seeds sown in containers without lids can be placed inside a plastic bag that is propped open with a popsicle stick.

Use a good soil-less mix formulated especially for seed starting, and always use clean containers. Sprinkling sphagnum peat moss (not regular peat moss) over the top of the seeds, or pressing tiny seeds into a layer of sphagnum, will combat a disease called "damping off." This disease kills new seedlings, cutting them off right at the soil line. (Always handle sphagnum peat with surgical gloves because it can cause infections of the fingernails.) Make a label for each container, including plant name, date planted, and source. I recycle plastic labels from bedding plants by writing on the back with an indelible pen.

I usually give my seeds light from the time I rise until bedtime, and this seems to work. As long as seed containers are in their plastic covers, they probably won't require extra water. If they do seem dry, don't water the top of the container. Instead, pour water into a plastic tray under the container and allow it to soak up from the bottom.

When two true leaves appear (the first leaves are round, fleshy cotyledon leaves and totally unlike the true leaves of the plant), the plants are ready to be transplanted. I use old bedding plant containers and trays that have been rinsed out in a ten percent bleach solution to kill bacteria.

Grasp the plant gently by a leaf, never the tender stem,

and carefully separate the roots from the group. Using a tool such as a spoon or the end of a flat stick, move two plants to each cup in the transplant tray. At this point, you may begin giving the transplants a weakened fertilizer solution each time you water. When they are large enough to plant outside, they should be acclimated to weather outdoors by taking them out during the day for several days and leaving them in a sheltered spot. Bring them back indoors at night until they are hardened off and ready to plant in the garden, usually about a week.

Evening or an overcast day is the best time to transplant. To protect the plants from cutworms, wrap a bracelet of aluminum foil around the tender stems extending down into the top layer of soil. As you can see, the life of a new seedling is fraught with peril. You weep when one is lost and rejoice in one that makes it.

Most years I've started seeds indoors this way. I got enough good plants to keep me trying, but I also lost many that grew too tall and leggy or that I forgot to water. And there's nothing sadder than a new seedling that has keeled over from thirst and your negligence. It is usually fatal.

I've procrastinated so long this year that I am starting my seeds outside. All the preparations are still the same. Seeds will have natural instead of artificial light. They could also provide a tasty meal for slugs, pill bugs, or birds. That's why I cover each container of planted seeds with a plastic bag to protect them from this scary world. After the seeds germinate, I remove the plastic cover and try to find room to fit them on my potting bench instead of leaving them on the ground. However, once they are transplanted into larger containers, the plants are on their own and must finish growing to transplant size while resting on the ground.

Slugs can be lured into drowning themselves in a drunken delirium if you set out jar lids of beer. Otherwise, you can dispose of them less compassionately after catching them in old grapefruit rinds turned upside down. If birds or rabbits are a problem, a cover of netting can help.

Since I never got around to ordering seeds this year, I'm planting old packets of seeds instead. These have been stored in plastic bags, tucked inside a metal container that I pushed to the furthest reaches of my refrigerator. Opening the large tin, I found all kinds of seed goodies — vegetables, annuals, perennials, and vines. Many came from the seed exchanges of the Hardy Plant Society/Mid-Atlantic Group, the Royal Horticultural Society, or the American Horticultural Society.

Other seeds were gathered from my garden or shared by friends. Waiting to see what comes up and survives is a grand adventure. Maybe I'll get the satisfaction of telling someone, "I grew these from seed."

P.S. If you are planting vegetables, please participate in the Plant a Row for the Hungry program, or any similar local program, and donate the extra produce to your local food bank or agency that feeds the hungry.

The Joys of a Garden Journal

"January 3, 1993. Call *The State* newspaper — a momentous event is about to occur! There's a swelling bud nestled in the foliage of the *Iris unguicularis* . . . I've had it for two winters and this is the first bud I've found."

These words from my garden journal are followed by a smug comment about the importance of checking the garden every day. After a week of rain, the entry for January 12 reads, "Well, so much for checking the garden every day. I missed the iris." A garden journal records the trials and triumphs of a gardener's life. You win some; you lose some.

Why keep a journal anyway? It has been fashionable at least since Thomas Jefferson kept such meticulous records of his experiments with vegetables and flowers at Monticello, information that greatly expanded our horticultural knowledge. One of the best Southern diarists of our time was the beloved Elizabeth Lawrence. In her book, *A Southern Garden*, she gave the earliest and latest dates of first bloom, as well as the length of bloom, for an amazing list of garden plants. I have referred to her chart many times for information.

As January is a good month for resolutions, I hereby resolve to write more often in my garden journal. While many gardeners jot notes on their Master Gardener Calendar, I have kept mine in a notebook. Dating back ten years, it is mostly a diary of observations made walking through my garden, including what's in bloom, what looks good or doesn't, and how that shrub my husband moved at least three times seems to be happy at last. By now I have my plants so well trained that they practically leap out of the ground when the wheelbarrow rolls by.

I also keep lists of plants and bulbs that I order, where I planted them, and how they performed. Don't trust your memory or those little plastic markers in the ground. Squirrels dig them up with alarming speed. As Master Gardener Val Hutchinson says, "You think you'll never forget that plant and where you planted it, but you will." When I think of all the lily bulbs that would have been saved if I'd only made a simple sketch of the bed and located the bulbs on it. Several other gardening friends talked with me about how and why they keep garden journals. Local gardener Eleanor Varner describes herself as a "record keeper from way back." She's been keeping her garden journal for four years. In it, she includes lists of plants that she purchased and their prices, where she transplanted things and how they worked, and what kind of fertilizer she used. She enjoys reading her journal throughout the year and gets out the old ones for comparison.

Although gardener Gerry Ballou has been keeping her journal for only two years, she has already seen its usefulness. Hers is divided into months with notes about tasks that need to be done. In page divider pockets she saves the tags of the bulbs she and husband Bill got in Holland and a record of where she planted them. She also keeps receipts of larger purchases.

My neighbor Dean Cecil has a young garden. From its beginning, she has been keeping notes about where she planted things. One of her first observations has been how quickly plants grow. This makes her more careful where she plants things that have the potential to outgrow their spaces too soon. In side pockets, she tucks packets of seeds and plant nametags.

The most diligent garden journal keeper I know is Fran Bull, who has been maintaining detailed records of her garden for more than ten years. Actually, she keeps two! One journal is in notebook form and includes plants she is studying as she grows them, allowing at least a page per plant. "I write very detailed descriptions of everything I do to a plant I'm starting from seed," she says, "how I prepared them for planting, when I planted them, when they came up, and how they performed." If it's a vegetable variety, she records how her family liked it. "Once I get to know a plant, I don't need to keep records on it anymore," she says. These research pages become part of her reference manual from which she helps other gardeners.

Fran's other journal is a diary of what happened in the garden week by week. "If you want to know what the garden was like on June 5 five years ago, I can tell you. In summer I might write a page for each week; in winter I might not write anything." Her husband, Walter, on the other hand, has his own kind of garden journal. He just takes pictures of his garden and puts them in an album; no words, just photos!

If you have been inspired to start your own journal, here's a list of things you can include in your very own gardening book:

1. Lists of plants and where you bought them
2. Sketches of garden beds showing where you planted things
3. Seasonal evaluations of plant performance
4. Germination information on seeds
5. Records of vegetable harvests and what the best varieties were
6. A record of expenses, for property valuation
7. A calendar of garden chores
8. A list of bloom dates
9. A list of frost dates and other weather information
10. Clippings of relevant articles
11. Photos taken of the garden or specific plants
12. Little essays rhapsodizing about how wonderful your garden was on a particular day

Winter's Little Treasures

At this time of year, anyone who drives by my garden is likely to get a view of my backside, with my hands and knees on the ground. Once in a while, I even lie down on my stomach to get a closer view of things. "What in the world is she doing?" wonders the passerby.

Let me solve the mystery for you. I am checking out winter's little treasures. Don't ask me why so many of the dearest winter flowers are so small. Perhaps it's because this is the only time of year that you can really appreciate them. All the show-offs from summer and fall have gone to sleep for the winter. But a clump of crocuses in January is just as exciting as a field of daffodils in February or March, or a shower of rose petals in May. You just have to adjust your perspective.

I have been observing the white crocus (*Crocus sieberi* 'Bowles' White') I planted last fall. The blooms are snow white and so delicate that I fear to touch them. There is a flush of butter yellow in their centers and I am intrigued. Into the house for my 10x hand lens I go (inexpensive, and for sale at college bookstores). If you've never looked at a tiny flower with a hand lens, or a strong magnifying glass, you are missing a chance to see a miracle. The intricacies of color and form will amaze you.

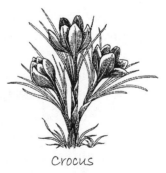

Crocus

Inside that golden throat is a three-pronged orange pistil with flared tips to receive pollen. This is the female part of the flower. The stamens, or male parts, which produce the pollen, are three little structures surrounding the pistil.

You do know that flowers have sex? Usually, it is with the help of an insect that brushes against the stamens of that flower or another flower, inadvertently picking up pollen on its body while collecting nectar. When it exits, it may leave some of the pollen on the pistil of that flower or the next one it visits. This is how many flowers reproduce and also how new varieties can result from cross-pollination as the insect moves from one flower to another.

The end result is the formation of seeds that will drop to the ground. The wind may carry them to other places, where they will grow to be like one parent plant or become a new variety made from two different plants.

After looking at the crocus up close, I was hooked. I went all over the garden checking for small flowers to examine. Have you ever looked into the heart of a viola? It's an incredibly beautiful sight.

A late-blooming flower of *Ceratostigma willmottianum*, commonly called Chinese plumbago, beckons next. I find that the baby-blue petals are suffused with a gorgeous pink, and the center vein and throat of the flower are also pink. Even the stamens are pink, but to the casual observer, this would be just a small five-petaled blue flower.

In a bed close to the street, there is a clump of Algerian iris (*Iris unguicularis*) that I check regularly this time of year for small blue flowers. This is another down-on-your-knees plant. I marvel at the complexities of this perfect deep-blue miniature iris. I carefully feel the foliage, seeking little swellings that indicate a new bud forming. This year it looks as though I may get several blooms instead of just one. Maybe at last it is settling in permanently. Margot Rochester suggests putting this little treasure "where you'll almost step on it, so you won't overlook it."

The flowers on many of the trees and shrubs that bloom in winter are small. (Camellias are the obvious exception.)

The autumn-flowering cherry (*Prunus* x *subhirtella* 'Autumnalis') we planted last summer is in bloom with repeat flushes of soft pink flowers. Close up, you can tell that the flowers are actually white with just a touch of pink on the petals, but the long corolla tube that supports the bloom is a rosy burgundy. The overall effect is a pink blooming tree. To give the tree a more open and spreading shape, we suspended water-filled, plastic milk jugs and soft drink containers from the young tree's larger branches. While removing the admittedly unsightly weights, I seemed to have heard audible sighs of relief. Did they come from the tree or from my neighbors?

Another tree with small flowers blooming now is the flowering apricot (*Prunus mume*). My tree is the cultivar 'Peggy Clark', which covers itself with fragrant pink cap-shaped flowers for several weeks.

The winter honeysuckle (*Lonicera fragrantissima*), a large shrub, will be blooming soon. You may not notice the little waxy white and yellow flowers, but you will certainly smell their sweet citrusy fragrance all over the garden.

On a chairside table in the backyard, I have planted a rectangular trough with purple sweet alyssum, purple violas, tufts of moss, and tiny sedums with purple edges. Underneath are little bulbs, such as white snowdrops, crocuses, and miniature daffodils and tulips, whose blooms should sequence through the next month or so. The crocuses are the first to appear, coming up now. I have already declared this trough planting a success. Sitting in the garden chair next to it is a joy.

Other little flowers to watch now include those of English daisies (*Bellis perennis*), wintersweet (*Chimonanthus praecox*), winter jasmine, witch hazels, and the heavenly fragrant little pink-and-white clusters of blooms of the winter daphne (*Daphne odora*).

The key to enjoying all these winter treasures is to become a keen observer. Ben Jonson, the English dramatist, must also have been a gardener. Words he wrote some four hundred years ago still ring true today: "In small proportions we just beauties see, And in short measures life may perfect be."

The Garden in Winter

Winter is often the forgotten garden season. I walked around my garden recently looking for signs of life. I knew if I looked closely, I would find evidence of nature's quiet stirrings.

Pulling back the dead leaves around several perennials, I discovered little crowns of green ready to grow again. Under the dogwood tree, little blades of narcissuses were pushing up through the 'Catlin's Giant' ajuga, which has turned a glowing purple in the winter sun. As frigid as our weather has been, fragile-looking bulb foliage is coming up everywhere, signaling spring's approach. It's almost as if they know it's January and don't want to disappoint us by arriving late.

After reading and thinking a lot about winter gardening, I've come to agree with an English gardener quoted in Rosemary Verey's book, *The Garden in Winter*: "The charms of the winter garden have to be achieved consciously." In other words, a beautiful winter garden doesn't just happen. You have to plan and plant it.

The first key to a successful winter garden is a strong structure. While it's fairly easy in summer to plant colorful annuals to divert attention from structural weaknesses, in winter a garden's deficiencies are laid bare. Good evergreen background trees and shrubs are needed to focus attention on deciduous plants in the foreground. Walls, fences, and hedges enclose the garden. Hardscape, such as paths, steps, arbors, and pergolas, reveal the way movement should flow. Well-defined bed edgings and the placement of statuary, benches, and other focal points give the garden a sense of order.

Fortunately, we live in a climate where we can grow such a wide variety of plants. We are especially blessed with evergreens that help to hold the garden together in all seasons. Dogwood, crape myrtle, star magnolia, pussy willow, and quirky plants with unusual habits, such as Harry Lauder's Walking Stick and corkscrew willow, will shine in front of an evergreen canvas. Farsighted gardeners consciously plan for these effects when planting trees and shrubs.

River birch, sycamore, and some crape myrtles have interesting peeling bark in winter. Some cherries have bark that looks like polished furniture, while coral bark Japanese maple catches your attention with trunk and limbs of vivid orange.

Berries add color to the garden in winter. Hollies of many kinds provide a show for us, and food for the birds. Deciduous hollies are especially generous with their fruit. Other plants with berries include nandina, pyracantha, viburnum, and dogwood.

Winter is not without its flowers. Various witch hazels perfume the air from fall to early spring. Old-fashioned shrubs, such as winter honeysuckle and wintersweet, join in. Perhaps everyone's favorite winter-blooming shrub is the *Daphne odora*, which is beautiful in every way — foliage, form, and delicious fragrance. Our area is famous for camellias, which can bloom from Christmas until the azaleas start in spring. Choose new ones for your garden while they are in bloom at the nursery.

Evergreen perennials, such as the Lenten rose, bloom in late winter and hold their flowers for several months. Many new cultivars are available in specialty catalogs.

Little bulbs bloom in cycles through the winter and very early spring. A careful selection of crocuses can provide a parade of color from fall to spring. Narcissuses, like the paper whites, begin in December. Others chime in throughout January, with 'February Gold' concluding the chorus in early February. *Anemone coronaria* begins to spread its lovely, ferny foliage in January, before the poppy-like flowers that come later and last up to six weeks.

Finally, cold hardy annuals, vegetables, and herbs can be combined to create beautiful beds and containers. Visit your local garden center or a botanical garden such as Riverbanks to see how ornamental cabbages, kales, and lettuces can be combined with pansies, violas, snapdragons, rosemary, or parsley.

In winter, it takes an effort to see the beauty all around you. When well planned, a garden in winter will offer many delights for dreary days. Your efforts will be rewarded.

February

Spring Cleaning in the Garden

But, you say, it's still winter, isn't it? It's only February, you cry from your cozy den. As most seasoned Southerners know, the calendar doesn't mean a thing. Even if it's freezing one day, it may be balmy the next. Intermittent spells of warm weather in February are so luxurious, yet we gardeners know it's a dangerous time, too. A Japanese magnolia in my neighborhood is covered with soft buds about to pop. "Not yet!" I want to shout. A lurking freeze can turn its fragrant, pink goblets into a brown mush.

And there's always work to do in the garden. Most of the time, this makes me happy. Sometimes it makes me tired. My February reality check is to go out into the garden and engage in what my mother called spring cleaning. Remains of last year's annuals have to be pulled up, and perennials need to have the old foliage cut off. Many flower pots contain collapsed and slimy plants that were finished off by a hard freeze. The soil from the pots, as well as the plants, make a good addition to the compost heap, along with the leaves raked from the yard.

It's also a great time to weed. Pull up seedlings of oak, cherry laurel, or whatever happens to be the bane of your garden's existence. I spent a mild day recently crawling around under my huge azaleas and camellias pulling out little seedlings while the ground was still soft from melted snow. The ones that had eluded me last year had grown tall enough to warrant use of a shovel.

Another scourge in one of my beds is variegated vinca. It is so pretty I'm always tempted to leave some. When it climbs up into a shrub it makes a fine contrast with colorful flowers and green foliage. But I always regret it this time of year because it takes over the whole bed. It is best saved as a trailing plant for containers if you watch it and don't let it root in the ground below.

Pick up limbs and sticks from the winter. My garden had its share of damage, but now the debris has been carried away. Cleaning up the garden like this makes it look so neat. I think I value orderliness in the garden this time of year almost as much as I do exuberance of flower and foliage in summer.

The garden's hardscape and its layout are most prominent now, but you know something good is going to be happening soon. Imagining how that bare garden can soon be filled with color reminds me that it's also time to get in those orders for unusual seeds and plants from specialty catalogs before the spring rush.

Just look at those bulbs sending up their foliage! This is the time to fertilize them with a bulb booster fertilizer and to keep them watered. You can feed them again after they finish blooming to help them form next year's flowers. Remember to let the foliage remain on the bulbs until it turns yellow. Then it will have time to form flowers for next year before the summer and fall dormancy.

If you have any shrubs that need pruning or moving, time is running short. You want everything to get settled in before summer's heat comes. Forsythias in bloom and Valentine's Day remind me it's time to prune my roses. I do my boxwoods about the first of March. Other evergreen shrubs can be pruned now just before the growing season starts. Before you know it, the pruning cuts will be covered by new leaves. Remember to prune spring-flowering shrubs, such as azaleas, only after they bloom. Pruning them now would deprive you of this year's flowers. Plants that bloom in the summer, such as crape myrtle and buddleia, can be pruned in the spring because they bloom on this year's growth.

Winter annuals such as pansies and violas, kales, and cabbages should be coming into their glory soon, so keep them watered and fertilized. I talked with former Riverbanks Botanical Garden curator Jenks Farmer about other plants we could have planted last fall with those pansies and cabbages. He mentioned cardoons, the 'Red Bor' and elephant kales, the 'Giant Red' mustard, and the tat soi. All are getting ready to strut their stuff in March.

Our region's Master Gardeners Association president, Sharon Thompson, tries to plant some sweet peas about six weeks before the last expected frost. She says if she finds the time she spreads mushroom compost on her garden. If you have a truck, or a friend with a truck, this is a good time to put out compost to feed your garden this spring and summer. Mushroom compost is good, but so is the mulch that the city makes. And of course, if you have access to aged animal manure, you are lucky indeed. I'd like to have a truckload dumped in my driveway.

Val Hutchinson has been pruning butterfly bushes and other shrubs. Her parsley is so green "it looks like a little rain forest." Jim Bente has just brought in his pots of amaryllis bulbs, later than usual, but they're already sprouting.

My neighbor and gardening friend Dean Cecil is assessing her successes and mistakes from last year. "My plan is to start preparing my beds. I've recognized from last year's growth what I liked and disliked and am making some changes." She is preparing to move some large camellias from the front of her house to the back. In their place, she wants to put in something smaller as foundation plants and perhaps add some window boxes to the front of the house. In preparation for moving these large camellias, she has been root pruning them to lessen the shock of transplanting. By plunging a shovel into the ground all the way around the plant at the drip line, you will encourage more roots to grow into the root ball area.

She is also checking out her watering system and planning to make some additions, such as little feeder tubes from her drip system to individual pots or window boxes. If you don't have an irrigation system, this is a good time to add one. Think about doing it in zones. Turf requires a different amount of water than shrubs or flower beds.

People who move here from colder climates soon realize how true are the words of the legendary gardener, Elizabeth Lawrence: "There is no time for the gardener to take a rest before beginning again . . . in a part of the world where at all times of the year there are days when it is good to be out of doors, when there is work to be done in the garden, and when there is some plant in perfection of flower or fruit."

> A Winter Walk through Riverbanks Botanical Garden

Last Monday was mild and sunny. It was the kind of day that Elizabeth Lawrence would have described as one of "winter's sometime smiles." The crazy but wonderful uncertainties of a Southern winter allow many such breaks in the cold to garden or to do what my husband and I did. We visited Riverbanks Zoo and Botanical Garden.

I know what's happening in my small garden. I check it every day. But I wanted to see more possibilities for garden interest in deep winter. Anybody who assumes the grounds of the zoo and the botanical garden to be bare this time of year is in for a very pleasant surprise. We went about midmorning and had it almost to ourselves.

The interest begins at the entrance gate, where the silvery beige flowers and foliage of dried miscanthus grasses rustle in the breeze. Inside the zoo, we began our walk at the

Lily Pond Garden, looking at the beautiful evergreen plants that lend it structure in winter — tea olive (*Osmanthus fragrans*) in bloom, mahonia (coming into bloom), Florida anise (leaves fragrant when crushed), and evergreen groundcovers, such as pachysandra, hellebores, and *Rohdea japonica*. The star plant, however, was deciduous. Several large wintersweet shrubs (*Chimonanthus praecox*) filled the air with the heavenly fragrance of their tiny witch-hazel-like blooms.

We noticed the red-and-brown bark of bare crape myrtle trees. Containers along the path held colorful combinations of ornamental cabbages, kales, and pansies. A star magnolia (*Magnolia stellata*) was coming into bloom just outside the education building.

Leaving the zoo's grounds by walking across the bridge to the botanical garden, we had a breathtaking view of the river and the trees dripping with grey Spanish moss along the bank. At the end of the bridge, we headed into the Woodland Garden. Although it is too early to see wildflower blooms, the views through the winter-bare trees clearly revealed the Saluda River just beyond. Winter edits out all the exuberance of spring and summer; and allows us to see tree trunks, the dried honey-gold leaves still clinging to the beech trees, the green of Christmas fern and wild ginger, and the majesty of the huge moss-dappled rocks that populate the woods here. These visual treats are accompanied by the soothing sounds of the river rapids below.

Coming out of the woods, we entered the Rose Garden. While there may be no blooms now, the bare stems of the roses are bright green, and the ground beneath is covered with hundreds of lavender violas, large mounds of grey-green artemisia, and mats of silvery dianthus and green parsley. On an arbor a hardy noisette rose, 'Crepuscule', had a freeze-dried bloom beside a new bud.

Horticulturist Charlie Ryan told us to look for the mahonias in bloom. "There's also winter honeysuckle (*Lonicera fragrantissima*); paper bush (*Edgeworthia papyrifera*), with interesting buds about to pop open; and three flowering apricots (*Prunus mume*) on the driveway side of the reception center. And don't forget to see the 'Red Bor' kale with its really dark purple leaves in the Purple Border."

At the lower entrance to the Walled Garden, a feathery sea of dried *Muhlenbergia dumosa* grass begged for a sweep of our hand over its top. A gardener suggested we look for "some good combinations and textures" as we explored the garden. One of the most striking examples was the almost white trunks of the 'Galaxy' magnolias anchored in a dark-green groundcover of Asiatic jasmine (*Trachelospermum asiaticum*).

Three large containers were labeled so that you could copy the combinations. One held red 'Color Up' cabbage with 'Pink Shades' pansies and dinosaur kale; another, 'Red Bor' kale, 'Pink Shades' pansies, and 'Color Up' cabbage; and the third, 'Red Russian' kale, 'Goldshot' wallflower, Sorbet 'Purple Duet' violas, and Imperial 'Lavender Shades' pansies.

There are many beautiful evergreen hollies with red berries or yellow berries, but the holly that took the prize was a deciduous one, *Ilex verticillata* 'Winter Red'. It was loaded with bright red berries along its bare stems. To set off the picture, a mockingbird flew in and landed on one of its branches.

In this main part of the Walled Garden, three autumn-flowering cherries (*Prunus x subhirtella* 'Autumnalis'), were in bloom in different parts of the garden. Three large beds were planted with combinations of brassicas (kale, cabbage, and mustard) and purple violas.

A blue-green eucalyptus made a perfect companion for a yellow-leaved form of Hinoki cypress (*Chamaecyparis obtusa*

'Crippsii'). Everywhere we looked there was another showy plant, beautyberry (*Callicarpa sikokiana*) still holding most of its lavender berries, winter hazel (*Corylopsis glabrescens*) ready to bloom, the strawberry tree (*Arbutus unedo*) already blooming, and a Jerusalem cherry (*Solanum pseudocapsicum*) covered with large red berries.

My favorite plant by far was a magnificent specimen of Harry Lauder's Walking Stick, with its bare, tortuous and twisting branches that could make it a star in a horror film. Covered with beige catkins, it is in its element in winter. In summer, it's just a large green shrub.

There is so much more, but I hope this sampling will tempt you to go to Riverbanks, or a botanical garden in your area, in the winter as well as spring, summer, and fall. Good ideas for your own garden abound, so take your pad and pen, and camera along.

Rose Is a Rose . . .

When Gertrude Stein wrote, "Rose is a rose is a rose is a rose," it showed how little she knew about them! The number of different kinds of roses can confuse even the best of gardeners. There's much more to buying a rose than just choosing a picture in a catalog or selecting your favorite bloom on a potted rose at the garden center. It helps to know what kind of rose will fit your situation.

The most basic division is between modern roses and old garden roses. Many rosarians consider an old rose to be at least seventy-five years old.

Fifteen classes of old garden roses and ten classes of modern roses make it necessary to know what you are buying. If you want long-stemmed roses for picking, you probably want a modern hybrid tea. If you need a well-formed

Rose

shrub to plant in your borders with other plants, an old rose is for you.

Do you buy a bare-root rose or a container-grown rose? Bare-root roses must be planted in late winter to establish a good root system before hot weather. Container-grown roses can be transplanted into your garden any time of year because you don't have to disturb the roots.

Will you purchase a grafted plant or one growing on its own roots? Most old roses will be growing on their own roots because they are usually sturdy and don't need grafting. Modern roses are often grown grafted to a sturdier rootstock. A swollen knot just above the roots indicates where the two roses were joined. In our climate, we plant this knot, called the bud union, one to two inches above the ground. If it is planted deeper, you will get growth from the rootstock and have to remove suckers. You can get a grafted rose to form its own roots by planting the bud union two to four inches under the ground and keeping the suckers that sprout from below the bud union cut off. *Southern Living* magazine's website offers a good explanation and pictures of how to plant a bare-root rose by either method.

Classifications of modern roses that do well here include:

Hybrid teas —Probably the most popular, best known for large flowers on single stems for cutting. Most are grafted. Require spraying for insects and diseases. Flowers, not plant form, are key.

Polyanthas —Small shrubs with clusters of small blooms. Repeats. 'The Fairy' is an example.

Floribundas —Bush type, cross of hybrid teas and polyanthas. Blooms in clusters. Repeats. 'Iceberg'.

Grandiflora — A large rose with clustered flowers and long stems for cutting. 'Peace'.

Miniatures — All parts smaller, growing one to one and half feet, except for climbers. Look delicate but are hardy. Grow outside.

Climbers — Long canes to train on arbors or trellises. Ramblers are large climbers and pillar roses are shorter.

Shrub roses — A very diverse class.

Some of the classes of old roses best for the South include:

Chinas — First ever-blooming roses; one of parents for all modern repeat-blooming roses. Many flowers, disease resistant, long-lived.

Teas — Most have heady fragrance, large plants, heavy bloom spring and fall.

Noisettes — The only rose class developed in South Carolina. Repeat flowering shrubs and climbers.

Hybrid Musk — Good foliage and disease resistance, fragrant. Repeats. May tolerate some shade.

David Austin — English roses of old garden type developed in last fifty years.

Gardening as Therapy

Like to curl up by the fire with a good book on a cold winter day? Then try *Shovel It: Nature's Health Plan* by Eva Shaw. Not only does it make a convincing case for the healing powers of gardening, it also explains how to get started, how to visualize your dream garden by putting your ideas on paper before you put your shovel in the ground.

More people than ever are gardening. If you are one of

them, you already know how working in the soil calms your nerves, helps keep your waistline slim (or perhaps slimmer), gives you a good aerobic workout, helps to brighten your outlook on life or regain health. It may help you live longer, and it certainly feeds your soul!

Eva Shaw's garden contains flowers, trees, vegetables, and sculptures; everything but perfection. She has gardened wherever she has lived to produce vegetables and flowers. "Rarely in my younger days did I give a second thought to the health-happy conditions I had created in my life and the lives of others who shared my bountiful harvests. Then as events do, one led to another and I could see that those who garden were happier and healthier." Her book is the result of a personal quest to find out why this is true, and she invites you to partake in the harvest, too.

Throughout the book, Shaw offers wonderful words of wisdom from gardeners and naturalists down through the ages. Reading these words and thinking about them can be therapeutic, in and of itself.

"One who plants a garden plants happiness" is an old Chinese proverb, which reminds us that since time immemorial, people have found gardening to be a remedy for the ills that beset them.

A similar thought was expressed by the horticulturist Luther Burbank, who wrote "Flowers always make people better, happier, and more healthful; they are sunshine, food and medicine to the soul."

Flowers can be seen blooming year-round here in the South Carolina Midlands, thanks to our climate. Perhaps that's why it's so easy for us to take their beauty for granted. Speaking of flowers, author Iris Murdoch said, "People from a planet without flowers would think we must be mad with joy the whole time to have such things about us."

The conservationist John Muir likens our need for beauty

to our need for bread: "Everybody needs beauty as well as bread, places to play in and pray in, where Nature may heal and cheer and give strength to body and soul alike."

Rachel Carson, the naturalist, also notes the restorative benefits of nature's beauty: "Those who dwell, as scientists or laymen, among the beauties and mysteries of the earth are never alone or weary of life . . . Those who contemplate the beauty of the earth find reserves of strength that will endure as long as life lasts."

Those same people are, or become, optimists. Marina Schinz writes "To create a garden is to search for a better world. In our effort to improve nature, we are guided by a vision of paradise. Whether the result is a horticultural masterpiece or only a modest vegetable patch, it is based on the expectation of a glorious future. This hope for the future is at the heart of all gardens."

May Sarton puts her finger on the source of gardening's therapeutic powers in this hectic, modern world: "It's everything that slows us down and forces patience, everything that sets us back into the slow cycles of nature. [The] garden is an instrument of grace."

Get started now on the road to fitness, in mind and body. Take Shaw's advice and just shovel it.

African Violets in South Carolina Windows

I'm a yard gardener. Growing houseplants has never been my strong suit, but I can grow African violets. This African native is not actually a violet (viola) but rather a saintpaulia, named for its discoverer (no, not *that* St. Paul, but rather a nineteenth century Baron von Saint Paul-Ilaire).

Velvety leaves; generous clusters of

flowers in white, blue, pink, purple, or burgundy; and many different leaf and flower forms and colors offer great diversity. African violets take up little space in a partly sunny window and are very inexpensive and easy to grow.

In their native environment, African violets live in the humus-filled vertical cavities of rocks and enjoy a tropical and frost-free climate. We can deduce that African violets like humusy, well-drained soil; high humidity; and warm temperatures. This explains why they do well in pots with wicks to keep the soil moist, but not soggy, and are sensitive to cold drafts and dry air.

Light. Grow African violets in good light but not direct sun, which will scorch the leaves. East- and north-facing windows are good. To find the best place in your house for them, try various spots.

Water. The most important thing to remember about watering is not to overdo it. Keep soil moist but not soggy. Depending on the heat and humidity of the room, the violets may need more or less frequent watering.

I water mine once a week, but if they feel dry I water again. Always use room temperature or tepid water. Cold water will spot the leaves. Some authorities caution you never to wet the leaves. Others advise frequent misting to maintain the humidity.

My own method for cleaning dusty leaves is to give them a bath in warm water with a little detergent added. Allow the water to drain completely. Follow up with a liquid African violet fertilizer in small amounts each time you water. Sometimes leaves that touch the top of their container get soft and die. To prevent harmful salts from building up on the pot rim, cover it with foil or dip the top edge in wax.

Soil. Use a well-draining soil-less mix. One made just for African violets is readily available.

Temperature and Humidity. To maintain 65 to 75 degrees, especially in winter, group plants together or place them on the surface of moist pebbles in a shallow tray, making sure the roots are not resting in water. You may also mist them with tepid water.

Propagation. African violets are easy and fun to propagate. Cut off a healthy leaf from the middle of the plant, not an older outside leaf. Make a diagonal cut on the stem one-half to one inch below the leaf; allow it to self-heal for thirty minutes; and stick it in a small pot of soil-less mix. Place in a warm place with good light. When tiny leaves appear at the base, cut off the mother leaf.

Or fill a small jar with water, and cover the top with aluminum foil. Stick your cuttings through small slits so the stems are in water. When roots form, place the new plants in their own pots. If an older plant makes offsets, separate them from the mother plant and pot separately. You can also cut off the top of a plant that has become leggy and root it.

Pests. The main pest I've experienced is the mealybug. This soft, cottony-white insect lives in leaf axils and underneath leaves. Treat with Q-tips dipped in alcohol and/or wash leaves in warm sudsy water.

African violets make perfect gifts. Put the plastic container inside an attractive basket or a ceramic or metal pot, and attach a bow.

Mastering the Munchers

Is Bambi dining on your shrubbery? Is Peter Rabbit munching on your lettuce? What's a besieged gardener to do? Overpopulation and loss of habitat have caused hungry deer and rabbits to venture into territory they would normally shun. Whether you favor limiting the number of wild animals, or limiting the acreage under development, you find your prize camellias have been eaten, you want help.

Repellents. Most people begin by reaching for a repellent, such as Hinder® or Deer-Off®. Only Hinder® is listed as safe for garden crops, and you must apply it each time it rains. Deer-Off® works on ornamentals and lasts three months. It contains an odor and taste barrier that repels deer but is not offensive to people, dogs, or the environment.

One remedy reportedly deters deer and rabbits, and you can brew it at home. It calls for two cups of water, two old whole eggs, one garlic clove, one cup of chopped green onion tops, one cake of Fels Naphtha soap, two tablespoons of chili pepper or Tabasco sauce, and a gallon of warm water. Mix the first four ingredients in a blender until liquefied. Pour this in a bucket and add the other ingredients. When the soap melts, pour the concoction over your plants. Be sure you go six inches high, the height a browsing deer can reach. Apply this every week and each time it rains. Sounds pretty daunting.

Another downside to repellents is that you have to keep changing them. As Tim Davis of the local Agricultural Extension Service office points out, "Deer are vertebrates like us, so they have the ability to learn."

Other ways to repel deer include placing mesh bags of human hair around the garden, or hanging bars of strong-scented soap (with wrappers still on) from tree branches up to six inches. Others report that fertilizing your garden with blood meal or Milorganite® (made from sewage sludge) will keep deer away.

Predator urine is sold as deer repellent, but don't ask me how the suppliers obtain it from the coyotes. A barking dog, the next best thing to a natural predator, may discourage rabbits and deer. A good hunter cat may be helpful against rabbits.

Landscaping. You can landscape your yard with plants that are not palatable to deer. Bear in mind that deer may eat certain plants in one area while steering clear of them in another.

Flowers and Herbs. There are many flowers and herbs that deer may avoid, including yarrow, lavender, rosemary, thyme, Russian sage, artemisia, tansy, all salvias, teucrium, lantana, Marguerite daisy, wild mustard, dame's rocket, rock cress, all alyssums, candytuft, sea holly, globe thistle, santolina, verbascum, rose campion, lambs' ears, lamium, delphinium, larkspur, monkshood, foxglove, linaria, snapdragon, flax, bearded iris, peonies, pachysandra, epimedium, astilbe, ajuga, ageratum, poppies, lily of the valley, rue anemone, bloodroot, datura, jack-in-the-pulpit, and bleeding heart.

Bulbs. Try daffodils, onion, garlic, galanthus, ornithogalum, colchicum, and scilla.

Shrubs and Trees. Deer reportedly do not eat burning bush, buddleia, Japanese spirea, fothergilla, enkianthus, wax myrtle, junipers (but do eat red cedar), *Viburnum opulus*, magnolia, yucca, dawn redwood, mahonia, Russian olive, St. John's wort, barberry, daphne, and pieris.

Some gardeners try to confuse deer by planting things that deer find distasteful among the yummies. Others suggest planting the good stuff behind a screen of unsavory plants. Obscure the deer's view with hedges or covered trellises. If the deer cannot see what is beyond a barrier, he won't venture around it. Keep any tall grass or underbrush near your garden cut down to discourage deer from bedding there.

Fencing may be the only permanent solution. Rabbits can be kept out with a fence of hardware cloth extending at least two inches into the ground so that they can't burrow under it. To foil deer, fences made of wire or other see-through material must be at least eight to ten feet high. A solid fence need only be five to six feet tall. A deer that can't see where its feet will land, won't jump.

A three-dimensional electrified wire fence (a fence within a fence) is fairly easy to build. Your local Agricultural Extension Service may have instructions for this and other kinds of barriers. Also, Rhonda Massingham Hart's helpful book, *Deer-Proofing Your Yard & Garden* offers a very good overall discussion of the deer problem.

Finally, the homeowner may have to learn to make peace with his fellow creatures. Wildlife conservation consultant Yancey McLeod loves watching the deer and finds them educational for his children. Around his house, he plants things deer don't like, and elsewhere he plants food they do like. He believes that herd management, including birth control and controlled harvesting, is the best solution. Smaller but healthier herds are good for humans and deer.

March

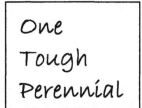

One
Tough
Perennial

Like sports fans, gardeners can't help but love the scrappy little underdog that somehow manages to overcome adversity. How else would you characterize *Helleborus orientalis*, commonly known as the Lenten rose? It blooms and flourishes under the dreariest and most variable weather conditions, when temperatures can plunge from the balmy low 70s to the bitter low 20s in the course of a few days.

The Lenten rose derives part of its name from the fact that it usually blooms during Lent, the six-to-seven-week period before Easter. As the common name implies, this hellebore is sometimes mistaken for a rose. Although there are many other forms of hellebores, the *Helleborus orientalis* is the one that has endeared itself to most of the gardeners I know.

This plant embodies the single feature that the perfect perennial should have: It is tough. On the afternoon before a forecasted hard freeze, I skip my Lenten roses when I'm out in my garden covering less hardy plants with blankets. Because they can take care of themselves and are bothered by few pests, these plants tend to be long-lived. My original clump of Lenten roses is more than twenty years old.

The flowers of the Lenten rose last up to five months and are very striking. The color combinations are stunning – purple, red, near-black, white, green, pink, and even yellow.

Lenten roses rise on stems ten to twelve inches long, with three or four flowers on a stem. The rose-shaped blooms are some two inches wide. If you are tempted, as am I, to cut them and bring them in the house, remember that doing so tends to weaken the plant.

The Lenten rose is often described as the aristocrat of the winter and early spring garden. Its foliage stays green year round. All the plant's parts are poisonous.

Another much loved hellebore is the Christmas rose (*H. niger*), which is not grown as much in these parts because our summers are too hot. There are many varieties of hellebores with contrasting and speckled hues. They have strong, shiny, deep green, evergreen foliage. The edges of the five leaves are sharply pointed. Use your heavy garden gloves when handling them.

Even though the white flowers of the Christmas rose and the multi-colored ones of the Lenten rose appear to stay fresh for months, a flurry of activity is taking place under those little caps. Seeds are forming in five little greenish-brown capsules that will burst when they ripen and fall onto the ground, where you may find tiny plants by next year. So if you want seedlings, do not remove the faded flowers until they have spilled their seeds. Seedlings pull up easily and make a nice gift for a gardener friend or neighbor.

Saving the seeds and then planting them in the fall is your best chance to multiply your Lenten roses. If planted in a well-prepared bed containing composted manure and lime, they should bloom in three or four years.

In nature, Lenten roses are found in damp woodlands and in rocky clearings, usually in limestone or chalky areas. They like north- and east-facing sites with partial shade and seem to do best when planted in well-drained soil. Heavy clays may cause them to develop leaf spot.

These easy-care perennials are available at local gardening centers.

In Support of Vines

Vines get a bad (w)rap from Southern gardeners. We've seen what runaway creatures like kudzu or Japanese honeysuckle can do, so we're a bit timid about the possibility of planting more trouble. I have decided that it takes a certain amount of gardening experience to appreciate all the different ways to use vines. So now in all my wisdom, I am enthusiastically embracing vines for many jobs in my garden.

As an Extra Dimension. Evergreen or deciduous, annual or perennial, mannerly or exuberant, vines have many uses. In a small garden, vines add an extra dimension. Where beds cannot be very wide, a vine growing on a wall or trellis in the back adds depth and richness. Where space for shade trees is limited, grow a vine on an overhead support (pergola) to provide shade. This even works on a deck or balcony if you plant a vine in a large container and train it onto a structure.

In a large garden, vines are useful because they can fill a lot of space, either trained overhead or onto blank walls or hiding quantities of bare ground as a groundcover. And in new gardens, both small and large, vines offer speedy results.

As Romantic Enticements. While providing shade, cover, and speed are important utilitarian functions, vines offer more romantic enticements of flowers and fragrance. When the Confederate jasmine (*Trachelospermum jasminoides*) blooms in my garden in May, I look for reasons to go outside. Let's have dinner on the patio; let's go out and play with the dogs; let's see if the pots on the steps need water – any excuse will do.

To use vines successfully, you must know how they grow so that you can support them properly. If they grow by twining their stems around a structure, as honeysuckles do, they need an arbor, trellis, or open fence. If, like clematis, they climb with the help of tendrils on their stems, they need a trellis or shrub to cling to. Ivy and fig vine have sticky projections or feet that allow them to cling unaided to surfaces like masonry or wood. Finally, some vines have no means of support and must be tied to a wall or structure. Jasmines and climbing roses are in this category.

It helps to know the ultimate size of a vine, too, in order to choose a structure large enough to hold it. Vines can hide an ugly fence or wall. Spray your chain link fence black or dark green and watch it mercifully disappear as you grow an evergreen vine like ivy, *Clematis armandii*, Carolina jessamine, or Confederate jasmine on it. One *Clematis armandii* will eventually cover forty feet of fence, making it very economical to plant. It also has small, fragrant, white blooms in early spring, about the same time as the Japanese magnolias bloom.

As a Groundcover. Vines useful for groundcover include ivy, Asiatic jasmine (*Trachelospermum asiaticum*), wintercreeper (*Euonymus fortunei* cultivars), and periwinkle, both the small and large forms. For a temporary cover for a large sunny area, an annual vine like hyacinth bean (*Lablab purpureus*) is a good choice. It has lovely spikes of deep violet legume-type flowers followed by rich reddish-purple bean pods.

Some of our most popular vines are the large-flowered clematis. Often used as mailbox or lamppost ornaments, they can also mix with shrubs. Choose a clematis, such as 'Jackmanii', that can be cut to twelve inches from the ground in spring.

As a Great Mixer. Many vines are great mixers, either with other vines or with shrubs and perennials. The classic social vine is clematis, the queen of climbers, which consorts

Clematis

happily with my Confederate jasmine as well as a climbing rose. Nothing is more romantic than the combination of clematis and roses. Choose a summer-blooming clematis, such as smoky-blue 'Betty Corning', to climb into a spring flowering shrub like azalea or spirea for two seasons of bloom. The clematis can be cut back every spring before the shrub blooms. Sweet autumn clematis can be used in the same way. I cut mine back to the ground every spring before the 'Lady Banks' rose blooms. Then the clematis crawls into a nandina and ever upward into the rose and finally into a crape myrtle tree.

Another autumn-blooming climber is the unusual climbing aster (*Aster carolinianus*) that will climb on a fence or arbor. It is covered with myriads of tiny lavender-pink daisy type flowers from October until frost.

As a Height Feature. Need a feature for height in the middle of a border? Try potato vine (*Solanum jasminoides*), in white or blue, on a metal form. Watch it, though. It can travel far, so keep it clipped. Two native vines that put on quite a show are *Campsis grandiflora* and *Bignonia capreolata*. Check out *Campsis grandiflora* 'Morning Calm'. Its orange-sherbet-colored, trumpet flowers are unforgettable growing on a lattice fence with a complementary rose.

Many worthy vines are annuals that can be grown from seed. *Ipomoea lobata* has small red-and-yellow blooms. Or try the subtle blue flowers of *Clitoria ternatea* 'Blue Sails', or the lacy yellow butterfly vine (*Miscagnia macroptera*) with its tan seedpods that resemble butterflies.

But there are so many more. (Someone stop me, please.) Once I discovered the versatility of vines I began to view every wall, fence, or vertical structure as an excuse to grow another vine. See for yourself. Before you know it, you, too, will be all wrapped up in vines.

A Flavorful Harvest

Where can you buy a tomato that tastes like summer and a tiny, tender squash so fresh it still has the bloom attached? Nowhere! But picture yourself standing in your garden munching on crunchy sugar snap peas, and you are already on your way. Whether your garden is half an acre or half a whiskey barrel, whether you want to fill a freezer or fill a salad bowl, all you need is a spirit of adventure and a bit of sunny ground.

The advice of two local Master Gardeners, Cal Shadwell and Russ Marsh, will help to get you started. These very knowledgeable gardeners have given many hours to community horticultural education.

First, you must choose a site for your vegetable garden. A level, sunny spot is ideal, but even a hilly site can be adapted by installing terracing. Russ manages to garden on a very steep site above the Saluda River by using railroad ties to build steps and terraced beds. On his only level spot, he uses long, wide rows, two feet wide by eight inches high, with mulched paths and drip irrigation down the top center of each bed.

Even in an urban setting, most gardens need fencing of some kind to keep out unwelcome animal visitors. Cal enclosed his twenty-five-foot-by-twenty-five-foot site with post-and-rail fencing to which he stapled fine-mesh wire to exclude rabbits. There are six four-foot-by-eight-foot raised beds with a center path between them.

The secret to the success of this garden is soil preparation. A soil test by your local Agricultural Extension Service will tell you what nutrients your soil needs. Even the red-clay-minus-topsoil that many homeowners inherit can be improved with the addition of compost. Whether you build a wooden or wire structure to hold it, or just allow leaves to rot in a garbage bag, you will have a fine soil amendment. Add household vegetable waste, garden clippings, and leaves. Russ Marsh scrounges leaves and straw off neighboring streets to throw onto his compost pile. He also adds chicken manure.

Be patient, though. Soil building takes time. With ground so hard that the tiller "just bounced off the top," Russ had to attack it in small bits with a pick and had to add sandy topsoil and compost. After ten years, he has a fifty-foot-by-fifteen-foot site in almost perfect tilth.

In addition to compost, Cal Shadwell adds organic fertilizer, such as bone meal and blood meal. If you garden in containers or small raised beds, you might consider using a purchased potting soil or soil-less medium. You can still add your homemade compost to these. You may also use a complete fertilizer such as 10-10-10 to give plants an initial boost.

How to choose among all the tempting things in the seed catalogs? Russ reports that he has grown forty-two different varieties of vegetables. Many Agricultural Extension Services provide booklets about vegetable gardening for a small fee.

Cal's favorite crop is broccoli, which he starts from seeds in January because he cannot find his favorite variety, 'Green Comet', as starter plants. Sugar snap peas are planted in February, along with 'Great Lakes' head lettuce, which is supposed to be difficult to grow in South Carolina, but which Cal has raised with great success.

No garden is complete without tomatoes. Cal likes 'Better Boy' and 'Celebrity', both of which are resistant to many diseases. You can tell this by the letters V, F, N, and T after the tomato name on the seed packet. This denotes resistance to verticillium wilt (V), fusarium wilt (F), nematodes (N), and tobacco mosaic virus (T). All tomato varieties will not be resistant to all of these problems, but try to get one that resists at least two of them.

Broccoli

Cal grows 'Kentucky Wonder' and 'Blue Lake' green beans on supports and says that half-runner beans also do very well here. Other favorite crops include 'Ichiban' eggplant, the new super-sweet hybrid corn varieties, yellow crookneck squash, and 'California Wonder' bell peppers.

Russ grows cucumbers in cages (another space-saving idea). In his raised beds and terraced plots, he grows herbs, green onions, cherry tomatoes, 'Viva Italia' tomatoes for cooking, all kinds of peppers, pak choi, snow peas on a wire trellis, and lettuce and spinach. After ten years, the cherry tomatoes, cilantro, peppers, and pak choi obligingly self-seed, along with many colorful annual zinnias.

Even in the winter, Russ has grown lettuce, spinach, and broccoli under a row cover fabric such as Reemay®. He found that he could pick some all winter, and by early spring have an even better harvest.

Russ loves to try new crops just for fun, such as male asparagus plants that do not set seeds; or 'Annie Oakley II' okra, which is shorter and faster maturing; or Burpee's tomato, 'Heatwave', which is reported to keep blooming and producing in temperatures up to 96 degrees.

Then there is always the problem of things that "bug" your garden. There are several approaches. Despite the fact that "insects seem to gravitate to my garden," Cal tries to use very few pesticides. He rotates his crops and does not plant crops of the same family in the same bed. He is trying a cover crop of cauliflower to help reduce the nematode population in his soil.

Using a product made by Tanglefoot®, he makes sticky, non-toxic traps for aphids and leafhoppers. Also in his arsenal are insecticidal soap for aphids and whiteflies, and beer and diatomaceous earth for slugs. For the uninitiated, beer is the finest trap for these slimy creatures, which will happily crawl into a saucer of the brew and drown.

Russ uses some chemical pesticides but only after first identifying the problem and looking up a remedy in the *Agricultural Chemicals Handbook*. He uses only the recommended controls for a specific crop and follows the directions explicitly. To keep fire ants off okra plants, Russ suggests that you smear the plant stems with petroleum jelly so that the ants cannot climb on them.

Cal and Russ use most of their produce fresh or give it to friends. The rest goes into the freezer to enjoy in the winter. They advise keeping records of your garden's successes and failures for future reference and drawing a simple plan to avoid ordering more than you have room to plant.

Russ finds vegetable plants as beautiful as they are tasty, especially when grown with herbs and cut flowers. Both agree that they do not garden to save money but rather for the personal satisfaction and pleasure of growing food that is fresher and more flavorful than any that can be bought. Cal sums it up, "One meal of home-grown sweet corn is worth the effort!"

Make Mine Perennial

I used to think that planting perennials meant that I wouldn't have to do anything next year. WRONG! I've since learned the truth of the words, "A perennial is a plant that, had it lived, would come back year after year."

While some perennials do come back faithfully every year, and even multiply, others may live only a year or two. All of them require maintenance, such as a yearly top-dressing of compost, dividing and replanting those that multiply, and replacing those that don't make it. The rewards are ample if you take proper care of your perennials.

Preparing Your Bed. Soil preparation is key. Have your soil tested by your local Agricultural Extension Service office. Some considerate garden centers will send it for you and save you a trip. The more time you spend preparing a nice deep bed with plenty of added compost, the better your perennials will perform.

Peggy Jeffcoat uses all the compost she can make and buy, but also adds other goodies to her rich, crumbly (formerly hard clay) soil. "I redo my perennial borders in the fall every three years," she says. "I dig up the whole area and add my recipe of alfalfa meal, cottonseed meal, blood meal, and bone meals plus sea kelp. I sprinkle these ingredients in layers over the soil and work them in, like I'm making a cake."

In perennial beds she is not redoing, she waits until the first killing frost and cleans off dead foliage, scratches in some alfalfa and cottonseed meal, and mulches with horse manure that's got lots of hay in it. "Every time it rains, your plants will get a drink of manure tea, and they'll be ready for spring."

Using Perennials. Before you buy perennials, give some thought as to how you will use them in your landscape. A garden of all perennials is possible, but it looks pretty forlorn in winter. To get the most enjoyment and beauty from perennials, try combining them with annuals, ornamental grasses, and shrubs. The annuals will fill in spaces in summer when a particular perennial is not in bloom. The ornamental grasses and shrubs will have a presence in winter and will add structure and fullness all year.

There are perennials for every season but very few that will bloom from spring to fall. For this reason, consider how they look when they are not in bloom. Is the foliage attractive? Does it complement other plants around it? Mississippi garden writer and raconteur Felder Rushing offers his formula for combining plant forms in a border. "Spikey, frilly, blobby," he says. "Have some of each kind for good balance."

Choosing Perennials. But how do you decide among all the wonderful perennials there are? One of my favorite ways to make choices is to read through the garden catalogs I keep filed in alphabetical order in an old peach basket. After turning down page corners and starring possibilities, I find myself with a whole host of unusual things. I look at the pictures and read about the plant's needs to see if it might fit into my garden. How could a gardener ever get bored?

Yet, I find it easy to become confused. The choices must be narrowed down. Several factors to consider will help. First, think of old tried-and-true favorites like daylilies, phlox, rudbeckia, verbena, lantana, and coneflowers for sun. If your bed is shady, consider hostas, hellebores, ferns, hardy begonia, variegated Solomon's seal, columbine, and Japanese anemones. All of these can be your garden workhorses, but try some new and different things just to make it more exciting.

Other ways to home in on what you want to grow include choosing a season for the time of most bloom, choosing a color scheme, considering your soil type and growing zone, deciding if or how to irrigate, and recognizing any microclimates in your garden.

Perennial of the Year. This year you could try the perennial of the year from the Perennial Plant Association. One good example is the *Scabiosa columbaria* 'Butterfly Blue', which blooms for a long time with round, tufted-center flowers of baby blue. Its sister, 'Pink Mist', should perform equally well. At one-foot tall, both plants make good subjects for the front of the border or for containers. They prefer full sun to light shade and need a well-drained light soil. They are reported to be trouble-free, and as a bonus, they are beloved by butterflies and hummingbirds. Now, who could resist a plant like that?

I must have that new ligularia I saw in a catalog to add to my ligularia collection. Another way to choose plants is to grow several different cultivars of the same species. I collect sedums, old roses, ivies, little bulbs, salvias, and hydrangeas. A favorite sedum is 'Frosty Morn', a lovely gray-green with white variegation. Many of my little bulbs are doing their thing this time of year. I have several new crocuses. My 'Whitewell Purple' crocus is outdoing itself, sending up one delicate blue bloom after another for the last month. I'm also happy with a new chrysanthemum called 'Single Apricot', a bright-red yarrow, and a new purple-flowered form of *Salvia vanhouttii.*

I often go to flower shows and botanical gardens, where I discover more "must haves." If only I had more ground to plant. Usually, something has to go in order for me to try something new. But go ahead, grow some new perennials in your garden. If you succeed, you will have more next year to fill in your bed or to share with friends. Ain't we got fun?

Look out your windows. It's spring! The birds wake us at sunrise with their happy songs. Each morning, I eagerly go outside to see what has happened overnight. It all seems to change so quickly now: nature at fast-forward. Anything not yet in bloom seems about to be. This is not a good time to leave home for the weekend lest you miss something wonderful going on right in your own backyard.

Hold Your Breath. By now you've guessed that I have a terrific case of spring fever. How did spring happen so fast? And can it last without a final blast from winter to curtail all this precocious blossoming? Now is what I call the "hold your breath" time of the year. Pray that a late freeze won't get the peaches, and get out and enjoy nature's exuberance while you can.

My dining room table is still covered with plant and seed catalogs with corners of pages turned down. I've placed only one order. How could spring sneak up on me like this? There's so much yet to do in the garden to get it ready for the upcoming season. To-do lists clutter the kitchen counter and the refrigerator door. As I nervously keep track of the daily weather forecasts, I must remember to take time just to watch the fern crosiers unfurl. I am tiptoeing through these last few days before April first, which is usually a pretty reliable last frost date for us.

A neighbor of mine has already put his tomatoes out. I'm not so fearless and will wait until we can really be sure it's warm for good. Otherwise, you might want to use some of those Wall O' Water® gizmos (columns of plastic to fill with water and put around your tomato plants for protection).

Remember What Has Worked. I find myself writing in my journal more frequently to record all the things that are happening each day. It's so much fun to look back at past years and compare the bloom dates with this year's. I can also remind myself not to plant certain plants again because they didn't do well in our hot summer. Some of my combinations in containers and beds are worth repeating. Next year I will be sure to repeat my combo of deep pink 'Jan Bos' hyacinths, pink-and-white 'Beau Monde' tulips, and 'Appleblossom' snapdragons from the Tahiti series. Reaching a height of eight inches, they are the perfect size for containers. I will remember that the evergreen clematis (*Clematis armandii*) blooms at the same time as the Japanese magnolias.

Prioritize Your Chores. If there is a cure for this feeling of urgency, how can I facilitate it? I begin by checking all those lists I've made and by prioritizing the chores.

Clean Your Beds and Add Compost. I've decided that job one should be cleaning out my beds and adding a nice layer of compost. The next best thing to having a pickup truck is having a generous neighbor who does. My neighbor and I rode out to a landscaping supply company recently for a truckload of mushroom compost and top-dress (a combination of mushroom compost and bark fines) for our flower beds. Landscaping supply companies have many mixes of soil amendments and mulches and can help you choose the right one for your garden. After cleaning the leaves from my beds, I have put down a layer of compost. In addition to feeding my plants, it will serve as a mulch.

Start Seeds. Next on my agenda is raising plants from all the seeds I received from two seed exchanges. Hope springs eternal. This year I'm going to get this thing right. There are new bulbs in the two shop-light fixtures that I have suspended over an old door resting on bricks. My husband rigged a heating mat for me by embedding a soil-heating cable in a sheet of styrofoam insulation cut to fit the table. A thermostat supposedly keeps the temperature in the mat at around 70 degrees.

I washed all my trays and containers in water with bleach added to kill bacteria. Then I filled them with a packaged seed-starter mix and planted one packet of seeds to each four-compartment market pack. I carefully watered them, labeled them, and covered them with clear plastic. And *voila*, they are on their own now. All I have to do is remember to turn the lights off and on and check the soil moisture. I have no idea what I will do with so many plants if they all come up. I just hope to get enough to make it interesting and worthwhile. Since about half the containers have baby plants in them already, it seems to be working.

Prune, Fertilize, and Get Organized. Next on my list is to finish pruning evergreens and summer-flowering shrubs. I have also set myself other tasks to get ready for the next phase of my garden. Fertilize the boxwoods and other shrubs with 10-10-10 or a slower acting 16-4-8 fertilizer. Visit local garden centers, nurseries, and farmers' markets to check out new plants. Keep lists of all the plants I buy and where I plant them. Note blooming times and performance in my journal. Take pictures to help me remember what each bed looked like this spring.

If spring is here, can insects and plant diseases be far behind? I am preparing for their onslaught by checking my supplies of safe and organic products to use. Many garden centers offer environmentally responsible treatments. Mail-order sources can supply you with everything from parasitic nematodes and wasps to a slug bait that is safe to use around your pets. Pictures of diseases and insects, shown in disgustingly clear color and detail in many mail-order catalogs, can help you identify your problems.

Check Irrigation Systems. Finally, check out your irrigation system to see if it works properly. I need to buy some soaker hoses to lay out in my flower borders. My overhead sprinkler system is fine for turf grass, but most flowers and vegetables do better with a watering system that puts water right at the roots and not on the leaves.

Visit Some Gardens. Now it's time to take a breath, relax, and enjoy this magical season. Try also to work in visits to gardening symposia and gardens, a great source of ideas and inspiration.

Listen up, sports fans for certain universities, and gardeners who want to know the latest trends. Orange is hot! Maybe it's time for a second look at this much-maligned flower color.

"You're not going to tell us to plant those huge orange marigolds," you say, "even if they are the latest color." I must admit that I have never had anyone request orange in a flower border I've designed; and I confess to having spurned the use of bright colors in my own borders. However, I began to waiver several years ago when I saw the effect of an orange-scarlet honeysuckle called 'Dropmore Scarlet' on a fence. Then a luscious 'Tangerine Beauty' cross vine stopped me in my tracks. The experiences made me an enthusiastic convert.

For inspiration on how to use these colors, I checked out the Hot Border at Riverbanks Botanical Garden in the summer. They use not only orange, but reds and golds and yellows, too; colors that seem to sizzle in the summer sun. These beds look good well into the fall because they contain ornamental grasses and late-blooming sunflowers, along with other hard-working perennials and annuals, such as tithonia.

The secret to making orange work in the garden is to pair it with the right colors. As orange is opposite blue on the color wheel, these two colors present a striking combination. Just think of orange impatiens and blue ageratum. Orange also works very well with the colors on either side of it on the color wheel, such as yellow-orange, yellow, red-orange, and scarlet red. A bed with these colors picks out all the colors of the sunset. To tone these down a bit, use lots of purple or chartreuse foliage. This can be found in plants like the sweet potato vine, both dark-purple 'Blackie' and chartreuse 'Margarita'.

Chris Rogers finds orange and purple "an awesome contrast." He showed me the solid-orange crown pansy as well as 'Jolly Joker', which combines both colors. There are orange impatiens, gerbera daisies, tropical hibiscus, and butterfly weed, and we were just getting started.

Garden center owner Rebekah Kline has used light-orange pansies with dark reddish-purple mustard in containers. She also combines orange *Zinnia linearis* with blue scaevola or purple petunias. Recently, she combined orange crown pansies and the large 'Majestic Giant Red' ones. She also combines *Zinnia linearis* in range with blue scaevola or purple petunias, and salmon geraniums with crown azure pansies.

Picture a window box overflowing with purple petunias and orange clock vine (*Thunbergia gregorii*). In the border, combine the 'Bengal Tiger' canna, which has yellow-and-green striped foliage and orange flowers, with a purple butterfly bush, a miscanthus grass, and old-fashioned lantana. Then let a 'Blackie' sweet potato vine scramble through it all.

Don't pitch those old-fashioned orange daylilies. They are just waiting for the right complement, perhaps either scaevola in front or *Salvia guaranitica* behind. In fact, the number of blue salvias that would look good with orange is tremendous.

Garden catalogs provide several offerings, including the evergreen Indian root (*Asclepias curassavica*), with orange, red, and yellow flower clusters. It blooms all summer, a lot longer than its cousin, the native butterfly weed (*Asclepias tuberosa*), which I love. The butterfly weed is always the spot of color in any summer wildflower meadow and can be purchased from nurseries. It has a long tap root that makes it practically impossible to move from the wild, not that you would even consider doing so.

You should also consider a fluffy hollyhock called 'Peaches N Dreams', an orange impatiens called 'Macarena', and a yarrow called 'Fireland'. I also found offerings such as *Lychnis* x *arkwrightii* 'Vesuvius', with bronze purple foliage and blazing orange-scarlet flowers. There were also *Cosmos sulfureus* 'Bright Lights', an orange geranium from seed named 'Orange Appeal', and 'Castle Orange' and 'Apricot Brandy' celosias.

Garden and floral designer Ruthie Lacey admitted "I used to be a snob about orange, but I've found that a touch of it just brings a container or arrangement to life." For orange cut flowers she likes pomegranate, the native flame azalea, the Asiatic and turkscap lilies, lantana 'Miss Huff's Hardy', roses, freesia, *Euphorbia fulgens*, pale-orange dahlias, celosia, and snapdragons, as well as the bright summer flowers of the bulbs of crocosmia. In containers, she likes *Zinnia linearis*, a shorter lantana, and dahlias for summer. Wallflowers and orange pansies add warmth to winter containers.

In my own hot-color border last summer, I used one of the annual salvias in a peach color with a red coleus that had a touch of orange and a sprawling annual with little button flowers in orange or red called *Emilia javanica*. Peach-colored 'Buff Beauty' roses, yellow-striped miscanthus grass, 'Bengal Tiger' cannas and yellow flowering cestrum looked good in the middle, with chartreuse feverfew, 'Blackie' sweet potato vine, and 'Duckfoot' coleus as edgings. It turned out so well that I plan to repeat it this year. I may add some 'Enchantment' lilies behind the burgundy-red 'Crimson Pygmy' barberries.

I hope this has convinced you to add the spice of orange and other hot colors to your summer flower borders. There's still one combination I'm not ready for, though. Don't give me orange and magenta together.

April

It's Too Easy Being Green

Well, it's over now and it was truly spectacular. The first wave of spring color has washed over our gardens and parks in the Midlands of South Carolina and is headed north. I wonder how many dogwoods and azaleas were bought during the two-week period when they turn most towns into fairylands.

Sadly, their blooms don't last long. Soon we'll be in the season when, to misquote a famous frog, "It's too easy being green." That period is sometimes called a "shoulder season." Like the calm between waves, it follows the peak blooming time for high-spring bloomers, such as daffodils, azaleas, tulips, dogwoods, crabapples, and cherries, and it ushers in the next wave of garden color, which will come from roses, biennials like foxgloves and hollyhocks, and other worthy shrubs we may not know about. Perennials will be close behind. For those of you who yearn for a longer ride on the wave of blooms than your azaleas and dogwoods can muster, I have some suggestions.

A few trees that are possibilities include the fringe tree, sometimes called Grancy gray-beard (*Chionanthus virginicus*). It can be a large shrub or small tree. The blooms accompany the new leaves in fragrant, white, fluffy panicles of flowers that give it an almost ethereal look, definitely a head turner.

Another small tree, this one also a native, which blooms now is the red buckeye (*Aesculus pavia*). Its palmate leaves emerge very early, and are followed later by beautiful long panicles of tiny red flowers. The fruit is shiny and brown, often carried around in pockets as a good luck charm.

The kousa dogwood (*Cornus kousa*) offers single white blooms that appear after the foliage, when there are very few other flowering trees to compete with it. Its beautiful strawberry-like fruit appears in late summer or early fall and makes quite a show.

Shrubs that surf the shoulder season are many. The native Virginia sweetspire (*Itea virginica*) is a large shrub that is good planted in masses where its suckering habit is not a problem. The racemes of fragrant white flowers and beautiful late fall color give this tree more than one season of interest. Probably the most beautiful form is the smaller cultivar 'Henry's Garnet', with flowers up to six inches long and even better fall color than the species.

Viburnums begin to shine now. Not used nearly enough by American gardeners, this genus is replete with beautiful and useful shrubs. The snowball bush (*Viburnum macrocephalum*), with its huge round clusters of white flowers, qualifies as one of those "old- timey" shrubs that never go out of fashion. But there are so many, many more wonderful viburnums, many of them bearing some of the sweetest perfume in the flower kingdom.

Viburnum

As University of Georgia horticulturalist Michael Dirr says, "a garden without a viburnum is akin to life without music and art." Many of the most fragrant viburnums have been crossed with the koreanspice viburnum (*V. carlesii*). My favorite, 'Mohawk', grows into a nicely shaped small tree, whose clusters of red buds are decorative for at least two weeks before they open into delightfully perfumed, white flower clusters.

Another popular viburnum is *V. tinus*, with its white winter blooms followed by shiny blue fruit. In March, the dark-green leaves of doublefile viburnum (*V. plicatum f. tomentosum*) emerge. They are followed in April by showy, flat white flower clusters that stand out from the foliage and add a three-dimensional quality. To quote Dirr again: "a choice specimen of doublefile viburnum is without equal."

Soon there will be lavish blooms from hydrangeas, either the more common mophead types or the airier lacecape types. Hybridizers have been busy with this shrub. There are so many new varieties that it's hard to choose. And don't forget the vigorous oakleaf hydrangeas with their giant white panicles of flowers that gradually turn pink, and their colorful fall foliage and peeling bark.

Even azaleas can extend the season if you use some of the varieties that bloom later. After the large flowered indica hybrids have finished in my garden, they are followed by a later- blooming pink variety called 'Hilda Niblett', one of the Robin Hill hybrids. Our native azaleas are often overlooked, too. Once you see their lovely open habit and smell their delicious fragrance, you will want to grow them in your garden. Try the pinxterbloom azalea (*Rhododendron periclymenoides*), the Florida azalea (*R. austrinum*), or the Alabama azalea (*R. alabamense*). Unlike the popular evergreen azaleas from the Orient, many of our natives offer colorful fall leaves, as well as flower colors in yellows and oranges, in addition to pinks, whites, and reds.

Vines, both native and exotic, can make late spring interesting. My native wisteria (*Wisteria frutescens*) is just beginning to bud. Although its lavender-blue flowers are smaller than the earlier blooming Oriental renegades, this one won't eat my whole yard. It is much more restrained. The foliage precedes the fragrant blooms and sets them off nicely. I have mine growing on a large arbor, where it mixes with the yellow form of our native honeysuckle (*Lonicera sempervirens* f. *sulphurea*) and the best blooming of my white climbing tea roses, 'Sombreuil'. By the time my Confederate jasmine vine comes into bloom in about another week, I will be able to almost intoxicate myself on all the heady smells.

Ornamental grasses are just coming into their growth

now and will soon add beauty, texture, and bulk to flower borders. Spring perennials making their appearance now include the native phloxes, a variety of different dianthuses (including the pinks, sweet Williams, and thrifts).

Remember that foliage on your perennials is even more important than flowers, because you will see it for a much longer period, so it should be handsome. Soon the long, hot summer will be upon us, and you will be grateful for a variety of colors and textures from our sea of foliage. It's not easy being green *and* interesting in July and August.

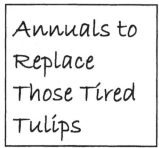

Annuals to Replace Those Tired Tulips

If you can drive by your local nursery or garden center this time of year without stopping to see what all that color is, you have more will power than I do. The sight of so many colorful flowers has the effect of a magnetic force on my car's steering wheel. Suddenly, there I am, walking from one area to another and making a list of plants I want. I ask myself where I can put this plant that I simply have to have? I'm sure you've guessed by now that I'm talking about all those flats of annuals just waiting to take the place of your tired tulips and passed-out pansies.

Annuals fit into many niches in your garden. In my mostly perennial and shrub garden, they help to carry the color along all summer, as many perennials have a much shorter blooming season than annuals. A display of annuals along your entrance walk or at your mailbox will gladden the hearts of passers-by. If you have a vegetable garden, add a row of flowers to cut or just to make the garden look pretty. Or try tucking groups of annuals into spots along the front of a shrubbery border for some summer color. Things get awfully green after the azaleas and dogwoods are gone. Plant drifts of the same color together to get more punch. Annuals really shine in containers, such as hanging baskets, window boxes, and planters of all sizes. You can have smaller pots of just one kind of annual. Or, you might try a large one with a pleasing combination of several plants, each contributing its virtues to a pleasing whole, perhaps an upright one for the middle, a trailer for the outside, and a medium fluffy one for the center.

One such annual is *Asteriscus maritimus* 'Gold Coin'. Its bright yellow coin-shaped blooms make it perfect for sunny baskets, beds, or window boxes. Another one, *Begonia* 'Pin-up', has more heat tolerance. It comes in six-inch flowers that are white with pink edges.

The trend toward plants with colorful foliage is still strong. For purple foliage, try the shrubby alternanthera. It looks great in many color schemes, especially pink and chartreuse. Many of the licorice plants are available, and the plectranthus comes in several forms. There are several helichrysums with fuzzy foliage and trailing habits for planters. My favorites include a gray-green one, a chartreuse one, and a variegated one.

Perhaps the biggest addition to the colorful foliage choices is the wonderful array of coleuses. Yes, there are still coleuses for shade, and there are now many coleuses that can take the sun. They come in more and more color variations each year. Because they must be grown from cuttings instead of seed, expect to pay a bit more, and be sure to ask if these are sun coleuses.

Trailing snapdragons, a trailing torenia that can take part shade, and a variegated green-and-white ground ivy called *Glechoma hederacea* add more choices for containers and window boxes.

The 'Purple Wave' petunia is a popular item. Unlike other petunias, it holds up better through the heat of summer. A petunia relative called million bells comes in light pink and a pinkish red. It works well in containers and hanging baskets or as large masses of color on the ground. *Scaevola aemula* (fairy fan-flower) and its cultivar 'Blue Wonder' are two blue spreading flowers that are still popular. Melampodium, with its small daisy-like flowers that take heat in stride, is a good bedding plant or large container plant. Other favorites are the pastel annual salvias in dusky shades of purple, mauve, rosy-red, creamy white, and pinkish cream. The bright red salvia is available for those who insist on a traffic stopper. Another good annual for us is bidens, in yellow or white. It's a fragrant sun lover for baskets or mixed planters.

Some garden centers use Fertilome®, a tomato and vegetable fertilizer, for their annuals. Its high phosphorus content promotes blooms on flowers just as it promotes fruit on garden crops. Most of the plants I have talked about so far like sun, but many of them can take a little shade, especially in the hottest part of the day.

Many garden centers find that herbs are very popular. 'Homestead Purple' verbena is popular, and it now comes in red, white, light pink, lavender, and dark purple. Still selling well are old favorites such as vinca, gerbera daisies, geraniums, petunias, and impatiens.

This hardly covers the whole selection of annuals available for our gardens. But don't forget seeds for other annuals. Most of the old-fashioned things, such as cleome, 'Heavenly Blue' morning glory, white moonflower, zinnias for cutting, and literally hundreds of others, are best grown from seed; and you still have plenty of time to do it.

Growing Terrific Tomatoes

There's nothing that says summer like a red, ripe, juicy tomato. It is the number one vegetable grown by home gardeners, and tomato sandwiches are just about everybody's favorite summertime lunch. The tomatoes must be home-grown, and the bread must be white, while several brands of mayonnaise have their devotees.

You, too, can enjoy this sublime treat if you just follow the directions of a few of South Carolina's best gardeners. Cal Shadwell, a Master Gardener, grows his tomatoes from seed. He starts the process about six weeks before the last expected frost and doesn't set his young plants out until April 15.

As it's just about time to put plants in the ground, your best option may be to buy tomato plants. Make sure they look healthy, are well rooted, and bear the name of the cultivar. There are zillions of different kinds of tomatoes. Cal's favorite is 'Celebrity', a good-sized tomato that is resistant to many ills that often plague tomatoes. "I also like to grow 'Park's Whopper–OG 50'," says Cal. You can tell which diseases tomatoes are resistant to by looking for letters such as V, F, N, and T after the name of the tomato. Each letter represents a problem the plant is bred to resist, and the more letters the better!

To fight blossom-end rot, another tomato plague, Cal says "you must keep the plants evenly watered. And don't give them too much nitrogen or you'll get all leaves and no fruit."

Cal works up his beds during the winter. "All year long I'm adding compost when I plant and I use compost as mulch." He makes the compost himself, adding worm castings from his worm bed. "This contains eggshells, so I don't need to add lime." He uses compost from his own compost pile, which no good gardener would be without.

To stake his tomatoes, Cal uses five-foot concrete reinforcing wire made into cages. "The six-inch grid is just the right size to get my hand inside," he says.

When the tomato plants make suckers, Cal removes them. My uncle, Emerson Scott, prefers to leave the suckers on his tomatoes to help shade the fruit from sun scald. He also prunes the tomatoes when they get to the top of the cage because he says he can't reach seven-foot-high tomatoes. He grows 'Celebrity' and 'Park's Whopper', as well as a few 'Better Boys'. One year, he tried one called 'Goliath', "but I couldn't tell that much difference. I am also trying 'Keepsake' tomato, a variety that is supposed to keep two weeks longer on the bush and six weeks after it's picked," he says. It claims to do this at no expense to taste; which is, after all, the reason we grow our own tomatoes.

Six weeks before planting time Emerson starts his tomato seeds in a miniature greenhouse he gets from a big discount store. "I also check the pH and add lime if needed, plus a small handful, per plant, of gypsum for calcium and my own homemade compost." Because he has such a large vegetable garden, he also uses city mulch and buys manure from local farmers to add to his compost. Then he broadcasts cottonseed meal over the whole garden. Concrete reinforcing wire is his choice for staking.

While Cal uses only organic methods, Emerson does spray fungicide for early and late blight. "I've started mulching with old hay and that seems to lessen the need for fungicide." He feeds the plants Miracle-Gro® or a similar product once every ten days to two weeks and keeps them evenly watered through a homemade soaker system, made with hoses and plastic drip rings for each plant. He also swears by fish emulsion, saying "Neptune's Harvest puts out a combination of fish emulsion and seaweed that is available at garden centers." Last year, Emerson had thirty-two plants and gave tomatoes away to at least fifty households. "My biggest complaint," he says, "was from several couples who told me it takes the two of them too long to eat one tomato!"

Lexington County Extension agent Powell Smith would approve both Cal's and Emerson's methods. Like a good gardener, he always gets a soil test done by the Extension Service for a nominal fee. He grows 'Celebrity' and a few of the super big tomatoes, such as 'Beefsteak' and 'Big Beef'. Well-balanced fertilizer, such as 5-10-30, at twelve pounds per 100 feet of row and three pounds of calcium nitrate per 100 feet go into the soil when he is preparing it. After the tomatoes start blooming, he side-dresses each plant with one tablespoon of calcium nitrate and one tablespoon of the balanced fertilizer every week. Plants are mulched with lots of leaf mold compost.

I hope this information will inspire you to grow your own tomatoes and not scare you to death. Actually it is not so hard. You can even grow tomatoes in a barrel or stick a few in your flower beds. My sister, Betty Stroud, is not nearly as meticulous as Cal. "I always start out by dropping a cow patty in the bottom of each hole. I've stopped growing them in tractor tires because the soft soil in a raised bed makes a perfect environment for fire ants," Betty says.

For those of us not lucky enough to live next door to a pasture, the best bet is to get some city compost or some mushroom compost. If you are successful and wind up with more than you can eat, remember that you can contribute your extra produce to Plant a Row for the Hungry, a program that brings in hundreds of pounds of fresh produce to local food banks, or to similar local programs.

Here are some basic requirements for tomatoes:
- Pick a spot with plenty of sun (at least six hours a day)
- Have the soil tested
- Prepare the soil well
- Evenly water each plant with at least one quart per day
- Buy resistant varieties
- Mulch to conserve water and keep down weeds

Camellias - a Southern Sweetheart

Sometimes things just click. After deciding to write an article about camellias, I called my friend, fellow former 4-H member, and camellia devotee Emily Wheeler for help. "You should see my mother's garden in Ridge Spring," she exclaimed. "I was just getting ready to go see her. I'll pick you up in a few minutes." Just like that, I found myself in a beautiful country garden filled with daffodils, forsythia, magnolia, hellebores, and wonderful camellias.

Northern visitors are often amazed to see these large, prolifically blooming shrubs in the winter. Long loved by Southern gardeners, camellias are natives of southern China and surrounding areas where the winters are wet and mild like ours.

Camellias prefer an acid soil (pH 5 to 7) with generous amounts of organic matter worked in, good drainage, a site with high shade, and enough warm sunlight to set buds for next year. Although many camellia aficionados grow their plants in greenhouses to produce perfect show blooms, the average home gardener wants something to put in the landscape.

Camellias are evergreen, fairly large shrubs that bloom (depending on the variety) from autumn through spring. This makes them very useful as an evergreen blooming screen, mixed in shrubbery borders with other acid-loving plants, or as specimens. I grow mine in a border/screen with gardenias and various hydrangeas. They may also be used as topiary or espalier plants.

Susceptible to frost damage in very cold weather, young plants may need some protection from freezing winds. Older plants are sometimes damaged but will usually grow back. Flowers that are open will freeze, but many others in bud will bring more bloom when the temperatures warm up again.

It is always better to water shrubs of any kind before a hard freeze. Just don't do what I once did and forget to turn off the water. The sprinkler ran all through a cold night, and I awoke to a glistening border of ice-encrusted camellias. Fortunately, the only thing damaged was my pride.

The flowers of camellias come in many forms. All are beautiful, but you may be drawn to a certain flower type: single, semi-double, anemone form, peony form, rose form, or formal double (no stamens visible).

Colors of camellias range from white through many shades of pink to deepest red. Many flowers are variegated, with colored edges, splotches, stripes, or picoteed. Variegation is caused by a virus, but it is not a harmful one. Some viruses are less stable than others, allowing flowers to revert to solid color.

Select your camellias when they are in bloom so that you know what the flowers look like. By visiting the garden center several times during the fall and winter, you can find early, midseason, and late-blooming camellias. Buy the largest plants you can afford. Since camellias are not as easy to produce as many other shrubs, expect to pay more for them.

A few rules will help you get your new plant off to a good start. The first is offered by Richland County Extension agent Debbie Hubert: "Plant it low, it will never grow. Plant it high, it will never die." This little rhyme is a good reminder never to plant plants too deep. That goes especially for plants that require perfect drainage, such as azaleas, rhododendrons, and camellias. Amend

Camellia

the soil for your plant with a mix that contains a high proportion of material like ground pine bark that is both acidic and helpful to drainage. When you finish planting your camellia, it should be a few inches higher than the surrounding soil because it will sink some after planting. Use a light mulch, such as pine straw, over the root area to help retain moisture.

Camellias are not heavy feeders but will respond well to one of the azalea/camellia fertilizers on the market. Fertilize them once or twice a year.

A number of pests can cause problems for your camellia. Scale and petal blight are the most prevalent. Scale shows as white, sometimes cottony, spots on the underside of the leaves. It makes the tops of the leaves look sickly and spotted with yellow. This pest can be controlled with a dormant oil sprayed on the leaves, top and bottom, twice a year, in fall and early spring. Another widely used method is to paint a one-inch-wide ring of Cygon® (diluted according to label directions) around the lower trunk in early spring. Other products are available to treat scale. Just be sure to read and follow the directions precisely.

Petal blight causes flower petals to turn brown. It's tougher to handle because spores live on infected flowers and can be transmitted from one flower to another, even from a neighbor's yard. Pick and dispose of any infected flower as soon as you notice it, and keep all spent flowers and petals removed from the ground underneath.

Camellia cultivars number over two thousand. Older cultivars such as 'Debutante', 'Governor Mouton', 'Lady Clare', 'Magnoliiflora', 'Pink Perfection', 'Daikagura', 'Dr. Tinsley', and 'Professor Charles S. Sargent', are flourishing in the Midlands of South Carolina, as are many newer ones.

I set my heart on a 'Herme' (pink with irregular white edges, early midseason) but could not find one when I called several local nurseries. All still have camellias, but when I asked for a particular one, the reply usually was, "We had a few of those but they're gone. We do still have plenty in bloom to choose from, though." The best plan would be to visit local garden centers now and maybe several times during the season and pick out something you love. You can't go wrong.

Your Own Rooting Section

How would you like to clone your favorite hydrangea, that special rose, your prized boxwood, or that azalea your neighbor always admires? This is the perfect time of year to do that by taking cuttings of these plants and others. What better way to save money and have extra plants to share with friends?

Right now, this year's new growth of woody plants is in a semi-mature stage — not too green and soft and not yet hard and woody. My variegated hydrangea was getting a bit out of hand, so I pruned some of the limbs and made cuttings to root. To do the same thing with your favorite plants, follow these steps:

1. Read all the instructions *before* starting and save yourself some frustration.

2. Gather four- to six-inch tip cuttings in the morning from a plant that is well watered, not wilted. Using sharp pruning shears, cut just below a leaf node. Remove the bottom leaves from the cutting so that two to five leaves remain at the tip. The sooner you plant your cuttings, the higher your rooting rates will be, so don't let them dry out. If you are not going to "stick" (plant) them right away, store them in a dark plastic bag in a refrigerator or in a cooler with ice packs.

3. Containers must have good drainage holes. If the container is not new, sterilize it with a solution of bleach and water in a one-to-nine ratio, and rinse it. If you are planting individual cuttings, use a small pot for each plant. If you are planting a number of cuttings together, a small styrofoam cooler half filled with soil-less mix works well. Cover the container with secured plastic wrap.

   I root roses in a one-quart plastic nursery pot filled with soil-less mix and covered by a one-liter plastic soft drink bottle. Cut the bottom off and remove the cap. This keeps cuttings moist and prevents excessive heat build up. This is a good way to root roses.

4. Use a planting medium that is labeled for growing cuttings. Bags of planting mix can be bought at all good garden centers. Moisten the medium well before sticking cuttings.

5. Make a small hole in the planting medium with a pencil. Dip the end of the cutting in a rooting powder such as Rootone®. Stick the cutting so that the powder does not come off. Gently water the cutting to settle the mix around it. Stick multiple plants two to four inches apart in larger containers. Cut any overlapping leaves in half.

6. Cover the containers and place them in bright shade. Usually the plastic will retain enough moisture so that you don't need to water. Never allow the planting medium to dry out.

7. New growth is a sure sign that rooting has occurred. Test by gently pulling on the cutting. If you feel resistance, the cutting is rooting. When cuttings are firmly rooted, remove the plastic covers. Some root in three weeks, others take months.

8. Plant the new rooted cuttings in larger containers and give them a half-strength liquid fertilizer. Plant them in the ground in the fall, or if they seem too small, leave them in their containers until spring. Mulch to the tops of the pots with pine straw.

For more specific information on rooting particular plants, check a good propagation book. I like *Growing and Propagating Showy Native Woody Plants* by Richard E. Bir and *Manual of Woody Landscape Plants* by Michael A. Dirr. Now, go forth and multiply.

The Bulbs of Summer

Daffodils, hyacinths, and tulips are spring favorites, but we often overlook the bulbs of summer. Many can survive our hot, humid days while adding color to flower and shrubbery borders.

Lilies. Elegant and stately, lilies steal the show wherever you plant them. The Asiatics, with upright-facing flowers, are the first group of lilies to bloom. The trumpet lilies follow with their large and fragrant flowers towering up to six feet. Easter lilies are a form of trumpet lily. You should plant potted ones outside after they have finished blooming. Oriental lilies are the latest bloomers and worth the wait. Three to four feet tall, these exotic-looking lilies have blooms with curled, and often spotted, petals. The popular and heavenly fragrant rubrum lily is in this group.

Gloriosa rothschildiana is the showiest of the climbing lilies, all of which are fun to grow. Using slender tendrils, they grow up to six feet and have very strange and beautiful red and yellow flowers.

Grow lilies in sun or part shade and mulch them well in winter. Plant them six to eight inches deep in rich soil that holds moisture but drains well.

Caladiums. Caladiums are among our best plants for summer shade, with large colorful leaves in variations of white, pink, and red. They make perfect companions for impatiens when you plant impatiens that repeat the color of the caladium. Wait until the soil warms up in

Caladium

spring to plant them, whether they are bulbs, or potted and sprouted bulbs. In the fall, dig the tubers before frost, let them dry, and store them in mesh bags at room temperature. Next year you can plant them outside, or get a head start by potting them up inside and watering them to start growth.

Crinums. Crinums are old-fashioned Southern bulbs, often called milk and wine lilies because of the pink stripe in the center of each petal. The fragrant showy flowers appear throughout the summer. While there are hybrids in colors of pink to red, the two best known are each deep pink, 'Cecil Houdyshel' and 'Ellen Bosanquet'. In either fall or spring,

Crinum

plant the bulbs shallow with the neck one inch below the surface of partly shaded, rich soil.

Spider Lilies. Spider lilies (*Lycoris radiata*) have red, spidery-looking blooms on bare stems in late summer and fall. Other colors are available, but are slower growing and may be hard to find. Evergreen foliage follows the bloom and remains through the winter, making this a nice bulb to plant with daylilies. Surprise lilies (*Lycoris squamigera*) have lovely pink amaryllis-like blooms in late summer on bare stems that are also followed by evergreen foliage. Both thrive in acid, well-drained soil. Surprise lilies will also grow in alkaline clay.

Cannas. These old Southern favorites come in many more forms than the tall red ones that are mainstays of municipal landscapes. Cannas with distinctive foliage are popular, most notably the hybrid 'Pretoria' with gold stripes on green leaves. 'Phaison' and 'Pink Sunrise' have stripes flushed with pink and are good mixers for a perennial border. Look for more cannas in specialty catalogs. Cannas prefer a constant supply of moisture and rich soil in sun.

Lily

Ginger Lilies. *Hedychium coronarium* is a much-loved summer bulb for sun. Its white butterfly-like flowers on five- to six-foot stems are sweetly fragrant. Other ginger lilies are available and worth pursuing. You should plant the rhizomes of ginger lilies with just enough soil to cover them. They are strong growers, and you should divide them every three years.

Lily of the Nile. This beautiful plant is showy in containers or in borders. Its wide-bladed foliage is topped with clusters of blue or white blooms that last about a month each summer. The hardiest form in Southern gardens is the *Agapanthus africanus*, often confused with the tender *orientalis* form. *Africanus* generally has less than 30 small flowers that make up a cluster, while *orientalis* has from 40 to 100. Grow this plant in part shade in well-prepared soil.

Blackberry Lilies. The thin foliage of these lilies resembles slender iris foliage. It bears brightly colored flowers over a long period in summer and is easy to grow in good, sunny soil. Very showy black clusters of seeds follow the flowers, thus the name blackberry lily.

I've left out many summer bulbs, such as liatris, colocasia, allium, and crocosmia, to mention a few. Read about these and more in Scott Ogden's *Garden Bulbs for the South.* Buy bulbs at your local garden center or order from specialty nurseries.

May

Glorious Azaleas

The first blush of azalea color brings out the flower lovers. To think that a long period of cold weather and staying indoors could end in such a burst of glory is more than eager gardeners can resist. Everyone immediately heads to a favorite nursery or garden center for more, more, more of these wondrous shrubs.

A large majority of azaleas sold each spring is bought during the first two or three weeks, leaving only green in most yards when the mid- and late-season azaleas bloom. Did you know you can have azaleas coming in waves of color for two months or more? Don't despair because the azaleas are gone too quickly. They don't have to be.

Right now, the first of the early bloomers are coming on stage for the big production that turns our area into a wonderland for two weeks. Companion plants blooming at the same time add to the show. Dogwoods, Japanese maples, hellebores, daphnes, and loropetalum, as well as some late daffodils and tulips, really do satiate the senses.

The azaleas play such a huge role in making Southern spring gardens famous that we tend to forget that they came to us from the Orient. Azaleas are so popular because they have two very desirable traits for our landscapes. They are evergreen and they smother themselves with colorful flowers when we are tired of winter. We do have our own native azaleas that are deciduous. They fill the woods now and later with elegant flowers, often accompanied by sweet fragrance. They can be grown right alongside the evergreen varieties in a mixed planting.

Azaleas do so well here because we offer them a climate similar to the one in Japan where the evergreen forms grow wild. Azaleas like acid, humusy soil and high shade. Good drainage is critical. Pine trees overhead offer the perfect kind of open shade needed, but any site that is shaded by large trees that allow light to filter through will do.

North Carolina horticulturist, nurseryman, and teacher Jim Darden notes: "Most customers know azalea simply as reds, whites, pinks, or purples. Little consideration is given to bloom forms, plant growth habits, or plant hardiness. Many times the overwhelming beauty of the blooms in springtime causes the consumer to purchase a plant while ignoring many other vital qualities. The wise shopper will consider all of these things."

Although all azaleas are technically members of the genus *Rhododendron,* we think of them as two separate kinds of plants. All of the garden type azaleas grown in the South are evergreen, and all the native azaleas are deciduous; but both are azaleas to gardeners and not the plants commonly called rhododendrons.

Azaleas are divided into many different groups according to leaf and flower form, growing habits, cold hardiness, and names of the various hybridizers who have produced many hybrid varieties this century. The Kurume hybrids include small-leaf, compact-growing varieties that are hardy in a wide range of climates. Among these early bloomers are 'Coral Bells', 'Snow', 'Pink Pearl', 'Hinode-giri', and 'Salmon Beauty'.

The best-loved azaleas in the South are the Southern indica hybrids because of their large flower size and rapid growth. Many are also fragrant. Here in the Midlands of South Carolina we are in the upper limits of their range, and we can get some winter damage. Favorites in this group include 'George Tabor' (orchid), 'Formosa' (magenta), 'Mrs. G.G. Gerbing' (white),' Judge Solomon' (watermelon pink), and 'Pride of Summerville' (orange/red). Most of these bloom in midseason.

Some seventy years ago, Ben Morrison developed the Glenn Dale hybrids in Glenn Dale, Maryland. His efforts pro-

Azalea

duced nearly 500 new varieties with a wide range of plant habits and heights, bloom colors, and blooming seasons. By crossing many different forms and species, he added more cold tolerance, larger flowers similar to the Southern indicas, and bloom times between the early Kurumes and the late Satsukis. Some of his additions were 'Joker' (white/red stripes), 'Martha Hitchcock' (white/magenta border), 'Margaret Douglas' (white/apricot margins), 'Greeting' (coral rose pink), and 'May Blaine' (light purple).

There are many more hybrid groups, some of the better known being Robin Hill azaleas, Joseph Gable azaleas, Girard azaleas, and the Rutherford azaleas.

With several thousand named varieties, there is a huge range of colors and forms. Red tends to be the most popular color, followed by white, probably because white goes with all the others. The range of shades in pink makes this the most numerous of the colors. Three very popular pink azaleas are 'Pink Pearl', 'Pink Ruffles', and 'Coral Bells', all of which are early bloomers.

'Salmon Beauty' is another very early bloomer. It is really a peach color and goes well with 'Pink Pearl', a soft phlox pink. Early bloomers in orange are 'Sherwood Red', 'Orange Cup', and 'Stewartsonian'. Among red azaleas you will find 'Christmas Cheer', 'Hershey's Red', 'Hexe', 'Hino-crimson', 'President Clay', and 'Ruffled Giant'.

The flowers come in single and double forms. A hose-in-hose form looks like two singles put together. A semi-double bloom will have much fuller centers than single or hose-in-hose blooms. And doubles, which are very full in the middle, are the most opulent of all. Blooms can occur singly, in clusters, or in very tight clusters that look like balls of flowers.

When you go to your garden center to select new azaleas for your yard, keep in mind the place you plan to plant them. If it is close to a building, will the colors clash? (No magenta against red brick, or late red camellias, please.) If you use them in a foundation planting, choose a small variety. Azaleas look best if they are planted where they can grow naturally. They are especially effective when planted in masses of one color. Or you could plant an early blooming variety in front of a later blooming variety to extend the season. Planted with camellias, dogwoods, and gardenias, they make a lovely shrub border or screen.

Remember to dig a hole twice the size of the root ball and amend the soil with half organic matter such as ground pine bark, leaf mold, compost, or well-rotted sawdust. Check the drainage by filling the hole with water and waiting to see how fast it drains. Have your soil tested to see if you have the needed pH of 5 to 5.5. Incorporate dolomitic lime to soil to raise the pH, and add sulfur or ferrous sulfate to lower it.

Set the plant so that it will be several inches above the level of the ground and cover the root area with two to three inches of mulch like pine straw. Water well. Azalea/camellia fertilizer may be used after bloom and again in early summer. Keep plants watered through the heat of summer.

Visit your garden center about every two weeks during azalea season to see which ones are in bloom. Plant mid- and late-season varieties so your yard will still be in technicolor long after your neighbors are plain green.

Harvesting Ideas for Your Garden

Where do we get gardening ideas? Everyone has felt that sense of bewilderment when faced with an empty garden space. What to do? I'd like to share with you some ways that I got ideas for my garden.

Many good ideas come from books, especially those with pictures. Others come from garden magazines and television programs.

I seem to learn best by seeing things "in person." The key is becoming a keen observer. Stroll around as many other gardens as possible. Whether at the botanical garden or in a neighbor's backyard, you never know when you'll spot an idea you can make your own. Seeing particular plants and the way they are used in a garden may help you to decide what to plant in similar spots in your garden. Plant combination ideas abound at botanical gardens and good garden centers.

You may be intrigued by a particular color combination. I was knocked out by an Irish garden border, planted mostly in reds with other hot colors like orange and yellow. Plants with reddish-purple or chartreuse foliage made perfect companions for those colors. I took photos and jotted down a list of the plants. As our climate is different, I knew I could never exactly duplicate that hot border in Dublin. But I did a little homework and came up with a list of red and other hot-color plants that I could grow in South Carolina.

When I travel, I always visit other gardens for inspiration. I first saw trough gardens made from an imitation stone called hypertufa on a Charlotte garden tour. I'd seen directions for making them in several magazines, but I decided to buy one that measures twelve by eighteen inches. Never having tried a rock garden, I made one, in miniature, with little plants that would have been lost in a large border. For spring I layered several kinds of little bulbs under a top layer of violas. As the different bulbs came up and bloomed, I enjoyed a new garden every week or two. For summer, I planted little rock garden plants.

Shards of broken clay pots can make nifty herb garden markers when you write the plant names in permanent ink — another garden tour find. A beautiful variegated shade plant pictured in a slide at a symposium caught my attention. I spent three years tracking it down.

The idea of using brick columns supporting a large cypress beam to form the entrance to my sitting garden came from a picture in a book. The bench in that garden is a Lutyens design I saw in England. A local carpenter crafted a wooden arbor over my picket fence gate from a picture in a library book.

After admiring all the gazing globes that Edith Eddleman placed in the perennial border at the J.C. Raulston Arboretum in Raleigh, I remembered the huge, round, green wine bottle we'd found at a roadside "antiques" store long ago. I retrieved it from basement storage, laid it on its side in a border, and voila! I had a lovely, transparent gazing globe.

My birdhouse was ordered from an advertisement in a garden magazine. A rose to climb my pecan tree was featured in the Wayside Gardens catalog. Another came from a cutting from a friend. The essence of making a garden is observation and imitation.

Remember, good garden ideas can come from many places if you've just got your antennae out, plus a camera and a note pad. As the Bible says, there is no new thing under the sun. But there are ways to change someone else's idea and make it your own, so keep your eyes and mind open.

Vegetables As Edible Ornamentals

I know envy is a sin, but I covet my neighbor's tomato patch. At last, it's warm enough for all those heat-loving Southern vegetables to take off. I can almost hear the tomatoes growing while I sleep.

Though I love my own shady plot, I can never find enough sun to grow a decent slicing tomato. Short of placing them in big tubs on rollers so I could stalk the sun as it moves along my driveway, I am canvassing all the available spots of sunshine in my flower beds to plug in some vegetables among my flowers.

The idea of growing vegetables as ornamentals as well as edibles is not new. When tomatoes were thought to be poisonous, they were grown in the flower garden. Now we may forget they are pretty as well as delicious.

Gardener and author Rosalind Creasy has written extensively on the concept of edible landscaping. Should I try planting a vegetable garden in my front yard? She suggests growing vegetables, herbs, fruit trees, and berries together with flowers for cutting in a colorful and productive display.

Some of the prettiest gardens in town are vegetable gardens. Cal Shadwell, a Master Gardener, built a wooden fence around his garden of neat raised beds. An arbor at the entrance supports a grape vine. Almost invisible wire inside the fence keeps out the critters and offers support for brambles like blackberries. The soil is rich and crumbly, the result of Cal's homemade compost and good aeration by his homegrown earthworms.

He suggests 'Better Boy' or 'Celebrity' tomatoes and 'Ichiban' eggplant. These red and purple fruits also would look good in my hot-color border with red, orange, and yellow annuals and perennials. I especially like the eggplant's purplish foliage. Rosalind Creasy suggests combining egg-plant with a background of cleome, surrounded by blue ag-eratum, purple basil, chives, and thyme.

Clemson Extension Service agent Sam Cheatham, who loves his Lexington vegetable garden, says there's still time to plant peppers, tomatoes, beans, eggplant, Southern peas, okra, peanuts, watermelons, and cantaloupes. His favorite tomato variety is 'Celebrity'. He also recommends the 'Su-per Sweet 100' cherry tomato, which I could plant in a con-tainer with lemon thyme, parsley, and cascading *Zinnia linearis*.

But my real heart's desire is for a formal vegetable gar-den like Rosemary Verey's in the English Cotswolds. En-closed by a fence, it is laid out in beds formed by crossing paths of assorted paving and edged with clipped boxwood. There are small fruit trees trained on forms, herbs for fra-grance and seasoning, and flowers to cut for the table. An arbor on one side (supporting a grape vine?) shades a bench for resting a tired back and admiring the garden.

How could you ask more of a spot of ground? Beauty, food for your table, and help for others, when you share your overflow with local food banks.

Consider the Coleus

I used to barely give the coleus a pass-ing glance. Well, all that has changed, and how! Among all the old familiar tender bedding plants such as bego-nias, impatiens, marigolds, and salvias, coleuses sing out, "Look at me. I'm new. I'm exciting!"

No longer relegated to the shade, coleuses now can grow in sun or shade, making them very useful. They are great for containers and the border. They make combinations of other plants work. Whether your color scheme is hot or cool, just choose annuals that pull out the various colors of the coleus you like. Or you can do the process in reverse and choose your annuals first, then find a coleus that pulls them together. Either way you can't miss because coleuses come in so many different colors and patterns.

Coleuses at Riverbanks. I called Jenks Farmer, the curator of Riverbanks Botanical Garden, to see how they are using coleuses. "We mix them with other flowering things that might have a down time so there will still be something of interest in that space. Gold is a prominent color for us this year, and we are using a lot of a pale yellow coleus called 'Moonbeam'. It looks wonderful with purple *Salvia gauranitica*. We also like the small-leaved 'Duckfoot', 'Inky Fingers', and 'Purple Wizard' coleuses. The latter is a very dark burgundy and it really runs. Another favorite is a big-leaved one called 'Blusher', with leaves five to six inches across. It's a purple and rose combination but on the pastel side," said Jenks.

A trip to your local botanical garden will give you lots of good ideas for your own garden. Jenks' associate at Riverbanks, Melodie Scott-Leach, recommends 'Blusher'. She also recommends 'Pineapple Queen', a yellow one with a little bit of burgundy. Some of these wonderful facilities offer cuttings to local growers.

Colorful Coleuses. Nursery owner Pam Baggett has thirty-six named varieties of coleuses in her catalog, counting Unnamed #1 and Unnamed #2. Pam grows all her coleuses in full sun, but says a few of them might appreciate a little shade. She thinks some of the chartreuse ones might turn a bit greener in the shade, but they are worth trying there. One of Pam's favorite plants to combine with coleuses is lantana. "Orange lantana with 'Purple Emperor' coleus works great. Or try pink and yellow 'Confetti' lantana with

'Shocking Pink' coleus and 'India Frills', a selection with tiny, deeply serrated leaves that are pale red in the center with ruffled edges of creamy yellow and green."

One of the most colorful selections Pam has is 'Sparkler', which has "deeply indented, medium-sized foliage, centered with soft yellow, deepening to green near the edges, and playfully veined and margined with rose-pink, all on deep pink stems." It sure sounds like a winner to me.

Other suggestions from Pam include 'Waverly' salvia with the inky, purple-black of 'Purple Emperor' coleus. If you don't like the mixed color coleuses, Pam says that 'Pineapple Queen', 'Pineapple Prince', or any of the solid chartreuse ones look good with rosy-purple phlox or *Tradescantia pallida*. Because of the different leaf sizes, shapes, and forms, you can make a tapestry of different coleuses in similar colors. Pam uses an organic 5-5-5 mix in her containers and a nine-month Osmocote® fertilizer. To root your own coleus Pam advises taking a cutting, dipping it in a rooting hormone (such as Rootone®), and sticking it in a soil-less mix.

Coleuses in Containers. Coleuses are used a lot in container plantings. Try them with geraniums and a sweet potato vine. You can mix different-colored coleuses with 'Margarita' sweet potato vine and Purple Heart vine (*Tradescantia pallida* 'Purpurea') for a very colorful groundcover in shade. My favorites include the little 'Duckfoot' coleus, especially one named 'Confetti'. Solid chartreuse 'Gay's Delight' is smashing with 'Purple Wave' petunias.

Growing Coleuses. Coleuses are so easy to grow. They respond to an occasional feeding with a water-soluble fertilizer. If they start to get leggy in midsummer, you can take good-sized cuttings and have another batch ready to plant in no time. If you find a special one, you can keep it over the winter by taking cuttings before frost. Cuttings should have at least three pairs of leaf nodes. Remove the bottom pair before sticking the cutting in a growing medium. Cuttings will even root in water in containers on your window sill. Coleuses are easy to grow from seed, but you are not likely to get the same plant that you had. Using cuttings is the best way. I hope I have convinced you to look at these old, yet new, annuals with a new appreciation. Now go mix and match for a colorful summer garden.

Hydrangeas — Garden Aristocrats

Slowly unfolding their beauty each day, hydrangeas begin blooming in early May and continue through the month. How I love them! The grand aristocrats of the shrub border, they are worth watering in summer and worth covering with a light blanket when a spring freeze threatens emerging buds. Loved by Southern gardeners for generations, they have been discovered by collectors.

The best-known species of hydrangeas is the macrophylla or bigleaf hydrangea. Most grow three to six feet tall but can reach ten feet tall and as wide. Although ideally suited to cool, evenly moist climates such as in England and the Pacific Northwest, the macs do well for us in the Lower South, too; as long as we meet their water needs and protect them from late spring frosts.

Macrophylla blooms come in two forms, named for their shapes. Mopheads have large, globe-shaped flowers. Lacecaps are relatively flat, with tight center clusters of fertile flowers and a showy outer ring of sterile flowers.

'Mme. Emile Mouillère' is often listed as the classic white mophead. Its height can reach up to six feet. For a smaller white, try 'Sister Theresa'. The ruffled flowers of 'Amethyst' open to a delicate lavender. 'Ami Pasquier' holds its deep pink color even if the pH drops. One of my favorite new hybrids is the dwarf 'Pia', which grows only two feet tall and has proportionately sized mopheads of a lovely pink that gradually changes to red. For a true red mophead, look for 'Alpengluhen'. Its flowers, according to the Wayside Gardens catalog, "evoke the famous sunset glow on snow-capped mountain peaks in the German Alps." It grows to about three feet tall and three feet wide. And if big blue mopheads still define hydrangeas for you, 'Nikko Blue' may be just the one. Its deep blue flowers hold their color better on a range of soils, although acid soil will produce the richest blue. It attains a height of six feet.

The lacecap hydrangeas look entirely different from the mopheads. The small center flowers surrounded by large frilly ray flowers give them an airy elegant look that works well in mixed shrub borders. 'Blue Wave' is a good lacecap type and readily available. 'Lilacina', a prolific bloomer, disease resistant and cold hardy, is one of the favorites of Ted Stephens at Nurseries Caroliniana. My favorite lacecap is the 'Mariesii Variegata', a large shrub with ethereal blue flowers that seem to float above the beautiful foliage of mixed white, green, and gray-green. Stunning! 'Veitchii' is one of the best white lacecaps. 'Lanarth White' is similar but smaller. It blooms earlier and is thus more susceptible to those pesky late freezes, so put it in a protected site.

Among the best species of hydrangeas is the native oakleaf hydrangea. North Carolina garden designer Doug Ruhren declared the native oakleaf hydrangea to be his absolute favorite. "If I could use just one hydrangea, it would be the oakleaf because it looks beautiful every day of the year." It is a large, dramatic plant with flowers in long panicles of sterile and ray flowers that start out snow white and gradually turn through all shades of pink and rose to the still-attractive dry beige of fall. Fall foliage is outstanding. In winter, the bare stems with cinnamon-colored, peeling bark add much interest.

Local gardener Jim Porter shares Ruhren's taste. He prefers the oakleaf over all other hydrangeas and notes that there are several fine cultivars of the oakleaf hydrangea. 'Snow Flake' has longer, double-flowered panicles; and 'Snow Queen' has densely flowered panicles that are held upright. The oakleaf can take more sun than the bigleaf.

Several other species of hydrangeas deserve mention. The cultivars of *Hydrangea arborescens*, another native, include the beautiful 'Annabelle', with enormous white mopheads that give a long season of interest. This is a cutback shrub. It can be cut all the way to the ground in spring.

Often seen in the mountains, the panicle hydrangeas grow to the size of small trees and bear large white flower clusters that arch over toward the ground. The old cultivar 'Grandiflora', often known as the PeeGee hydrangea, is a rather coarse plant. More refined cultivars include 'Tardiva', which blooms in September; 'Kyushu', a vigorous selection that holds its flowers upright; and a scrumptious pink called 'Pink Diamond'.

The climbing hydrangea (*H. anomala* subsp. *petiolaris*) has been called by some horticulturists "the best clinging vine." In sun or shade, it climbs by root-like holdfasts up to eighty feet in height. The way it holds its white lacecap flowers out from the main trunk gives it depth and interest as a wall covering. Slow to get established, it reportedly grows fast once it gets started. I have never been able to grow it, as it is iffy in Zone 8. In cooler areas it is magnificent.

The species serrata is similar to macrophylla but less vigorous. It contains the lovely cultivar 'Nigra' with black stems and small pink flowers. 'Bluebird' is drought resistant and vigorous. 'Preziosa' has a mophead flower that starts pink and changes to crimson.

All the bigleaf hydrangeas thrive in part sun (morning or late afternoon) or, ideally, in dappled shade. Protect them from hot midday sun and cold winter winds. They prefer a soil that is well amended with organic matter and not allowed to dry out. A layer of mulch can help to retain moisture but shouldn't be put right up against the stems. The oakleaf, paniculata, and arborescens hydrangeas can take more sun.

The acidity of the soil determines the color of many hydrangeas, including most of the macrophyllas. A pH below 6.5 will produce blue flowers, while a pH closer to 7 will give you pink flowers. To make a wishy-washy color blue, mix a solution of ¼ ounce aluminum sulfate and ¼ ounce ferrous sulfate in a gallon of water and pour one to two gallons around the plant in spring and fall. Do not be tempted to make the solution stronger. Dried blood meal will also intensify the color.

By adding lime to the soil, you can encourage the pinks and reds. White hydrangeas are more stable. All the ray flowers in a white mophead and a lacecap will stay white, while the smaller fertile flowers in the center of the lacecap can be affected by the soil's pH.

The prospect of pruning these macs strikes fear in the hearts of the most intrepid gardeners. As they bloom on last year's wood, they must be pruned soon after they finish blooming, allowing time for new wood for next year's blooms to grow and harden off before winter. Otherwise, just leave old flower heads until next spring (they help protect new buds) and remove them in spring, cutting to the first bud. To reduce the size of a whole shrub, prune it by thinning and shaping *before* midsummer. The easiest pruning principles to remember are to allow enough room for hydrangeas to grow free-form to maximum height, and simply to remove old flower heads.

Hydrangea arborescens ('Annabelle', for example) should be pruned to six to twelve inches from the ground in early spring. Oakleaf hydrangeas bloom on old wood, so they should be pruned only lightly. The panicle hydrangeas bloom on new wood (except 'Praecox'), so they can be cut hard in spring. No pruning is necessary for climbers except to remove dead wood or control growth.

Although hydrangeas are easy to root from cuttings, the easiest way is to bend a branch to the ground, put a brick or rock on it to hold it in contact with the soil, and keep it watered. By next year, it will have grown roots and you can cut it away from the mother plant.

To use cut hydrangeas in a fresh arrangement, soak the whole flower and stem in water for a day or two. To dry flowers, cut them when they have aged for about a month and strip off the leaves. Tie the stems in bundles and hang the bundles upside down in a warm, dry place, or put them in a container with two inches of water and leave them until they are dried.

Most nurseries in Columbia carry at least a dozen different hydrangeas. If you want to explore the whole world of hydrangeas, try some of the catalog companies.

Impatiens for a Cure

I'm going to go out on a limb and declare impatiens my favorite annual for shade. So what's the big deal? Everybody grows impatiens. It's as common as heat in the summer, but it also happens to be the number one bedding plant for shade. It comes in many beautiful colors, is widely available, and easy to grow. Now I want to be completely honest. I have an ulterior motive for promoting impatiens.

In spring and summer, many nurseries and garden centers offer a special mixture of pink impatiens called the Accent Miracle Collection. Goldsmith Seeds has put together this mixture of three different pinks, which coordinates with the pink symbol for breast cancer awareness. Money raised through the program supports research for a breast cancer cure. This effort is especially important to me because I am fighting this disease, as have too many of my friends and family members. Those of us impatient for a cure hope that we can help by buying impatiens for a cure.

Participating garden industry people donate at least ten percent of their proceeds from the sales of this pink collection to the Susan G. Komen Breast Cancer Foundation. This foundation is the nation's largest private source of funds for research dedicated solely to breast cancer. Participants in the promotion include businesses at each step in the long process of bringing plants to market—growers, wholesalers, makers of containers and tags, and retailers. Goldsmith Seeds, developer of the Accent impatiens series and sponsor of this campaign, also donates all proceeds from the sale of Accent Miracle Collection seeds.

Although they are best in shade, these pink impatiens can take a little sun if they have well-prepared soil and plenty of water. In containers, which need frequent watering, especially in the heat, using a balanced liquid fertilizer such as 20-20-20 once a week is recommended.

Impatiens in the ground need good soil preparation with lots of organic matter and a long-acting fertilizer like Osmocote®. These pink beauties can be combined with browallia and torenia, or any coleus or caladium that has pink in the leaves. They also look good with the green-and-white caladiums.

Good varieties of caladiums to use with them include the small chartreuse one with deep rose spotting, *Caladium bicolor* 'Little Miss Muffet '(my favorite), plus 'Pink Beauty', 'Carolyn Wharton' (pink veins and center, green borders), 'Candidum', and 'White Christmas'.

I love to use pink impatiens in the shade with ferns, as-pidistra, hardy begonia, and hostas. My favorite hostas are those with chartreuse leaves, such as 'Frances Williams' (large variegated) and 'Golden Tiara' (small variegated), 'August Moon' (solid chartreuse), 'Krossa Regal' (leaves with a blue cast), or 'Francee' (green with white edges). Another interesting combination is the pink polka-dot plant (*Hypoestes phyllostachya* 'Splash') with pale pink impatiens. A small shrub with pink-edged leaves, *Hypericum* x *moserianum* 'Tri-color', would look great with pink impatiens, burgundy-tinged autumn fern, and hostas.

Another plus for impatiens is their attraction for butter-flies, which love it as a nectar plant. Impatiens bloom from spring to frost. If they get leggy in the middle of summer, just cut them back almost to the ground. They will recover in about three weeks and bloom right up to frost.

Purchasing these plants is a wonderful opportunity to do well while doing good. You can beautify your garden and remind yourself of the importance of regular checkups and self-examination. Just ask around for these special im-patiens, and let's help paint the country pink.

June

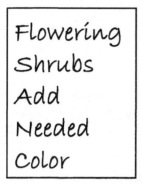

Flowering Shrubs Add Needed Color

Here we are in the lazy days of summer. It's too hot to work outside most of the time. Just keeping the lawn watered is a big job. What we need are more of those wonderful old-fashioned shrubs that bloomed in summers around our grandparents' homes. These are shrubs that, once established, don't have to be watered every day, and provide color in the garden when it is mostly green.

Take a look around when you're out and you'll see these treasures here and there, sometimes the only redeeming feature in an otherwise ordinary yard. Wouldn't it be nice to have some large shrub borders that cut down the amount of grass you have to mow? These borders could have many shrubs that bloom in the summer and add interest to the landscape.

A shrub that caught my eye lately is the oleander, a spectacular large shrub that loves the summer sun and heat and comes in colors from white to pink to red. Because of its size, it would have to be part of a large shrub border or used as a specimen. I've seen it planted in gardens with camellias and sasanquas and palm trees (something big enough to balance its size). It is carefree and long blooming. There's just one caveat. All parts of the oleander are very poisonous, so I wouldn't recommend planting them in a garden where small children play. Use them as a splendid background for a swimming pool or as a large hedge (all the same color, please), or even as a large container plant.

Landscape architect Elizabeth Rice says the Chinese abelia is a really good shrub for a large space, and it is the most fragrant of all the abelias. Butterflies love it; and it retains its whitish flower clusters into the fall when the leaves turn a lovely red. Other worthy abelias include the large, old-fashioned glossy abelia (*Abelia* x *grandiflora*), which blooms non-stop through the summer and into the fall with pink-tinged white flowers that are small but are produced in large numbers. Or look for the many smaller cultivars, such as 'Sherwoodii' with white blooms and 'Edward Goucher' with pink blooms.

'Francis Mason', a slightly more compact form of glossy abelia, has yellow variegated foliage in spring that gradually fades in summer. These shrubs are almost evergreen. If they grow out of bounds or become leggy, prune them back in late winter. They will still bloom the same year. Abelias also make good hedges, when allowed to grow together in their normal rounded shape.

Two kinds of loropetalum are getting ready to bloom. 'Burgundy' has purple leaves and pink flowers. 'Blush' is a bit more compact but has similar flowers. The tea olive (*Osmanthus fragrans*) blooms now and several other times during the year with tiny flowers that pack a powerful fragrance.

My friend Philip Jenkins, an avid gardener, says the Rose of Sharon (*Hibiscus syriacus*) in the form 'Diana' is just delightful with its big white flowers. "They look better after the Japanese beetles are gone," he says, only half jokingly. He also loves all the hydrangeas that are blooming now as well as the gardenias. "I've been to several houses lately where the whole garden was fragranced by gardenias. It made the garden seem so elegant."

I checked with the folks at Riverbanks Botanical Garden to see what's in bloom because I know they always have something unusual. I talked to Charlie Ryan, Senior Horticulturist and self-described "chief weed puller." One of his favorites is the *Indigofera decora*, a small deciduous shrub with pretty pink flowers and legume-like foliage. While the *Les-*

pedeza thunbergii may be too big for some gardens, Charlie praises *Lespedeza bicolor* 'Little Buddy' with purplish flowers and a fountain shape. The lespedezas can be cut to the ground in winter and will come back in spring.

In several places the gardeners at Riverbanks have used a native shrub in a cultivated variety. *Cyrilla racemiflora* 'Graniteville' (common name Titi) is about waist high, blooming now with white panicles. *Clethra alnifolia* 'Hummingbird' is also getting ready to bloom with fragrant white spikes.

How about a yellow blooming shrub like the *Senna corymbosa*, or the *Cestrum parqui*? The latter plant, commonly known as the willow-leaved jessamine, produces clusters of pale yellow flowers all summer in one of my borders.

Two of my neighbors have had success growing a pomegranate tree. It seems so exotic to see real pomegranates growing here in Columbia, but they are perfectly happy. There are fruiting forms that produce edible fruit, or make nice Christmas decorations when they are dried. Other cultivars are grown only for their bright orange-red flowers, so be sure to ask which kind you are buying. I have planted a dwarf form of pomegranate in my mixed border as part of the evergreen structure.

The coral bean (*Erythrina herbacea*) has tropical-looking eight- to fifteen-inch spikes of scarlet tubular blooms in summer followed by bean-like pods, which split open in fall to show hard red seeds. Steve Bender in *Passalong Plants* says not to try to dig up a coral bean plant unless you plan to stay all day. You'll have to plant a seed. Be sure to nick the hard seed and soak it in water overnight before planting.

I will never forget the first time I saw a harlequin glory bower (*Clerodendrum trichotomum*) in a public garden in Portland, Oregon. It was fall and I was seeing it after its star-shaped white flowers had dropped, leaving behind a red cup-like bract containing an iridescent blue berry (seed). Wow! Its heart-shaped leaves only added to its charm. Unfortunately, it was not labeled. I didn't find out what it was until much later; but I had stored it away in my memory, with the help of a photograph, and found it closer to home several years later.

Imagine a large shrub or small tree that looks like a pink poinsettia blooming in summer. At the J. C. Raulston Arboretum in Raleigh, I was bowled over by a *Pinckneya pubens*. It, too, can be grown here. With choices like these, no garden should be only green in summer.

I remember a perfume I knew as a child. It was called "Heaven Scent." Though I have no idea about its chemical makeup, its name suggests the heavenly fragrance of the Cape jasmine (*Gardenia jasminoides*). As billowing mounds of Confederate jasmine are finishing bloom, my gardenias are blooming. At this time of year, I blissfully float from one heady fragrance to another.

Although the gardenia is native to China and Japan, this beautiful evergreen shrub with deep, glossy green leaves and waxy, fragrant flowers in early summer practically shouts "Southern." Can't you just picture Scarlett with a gardenia blossom tucked behind her ear? In fact, the gardenia is named for a South Carolina botanist, Dr. Alexander Garden, who lived a few generations before a fellow, albeit fictitious, South Carolinian, Rhett Butler.

While there are more than 250 species of gardenia shrubs and trees, the one we know and love is the jasminoides species. Mike Dirr's *Manual of Woody Landscape Plants* describes twenty cultivars. One of my nursery catalogs offers eight. Of the double forms, it lists 'Mystery', perhaps one of the

Gardenia

oldest cultivars and easy to find. But I am intrigued by the cultivars that bloom longer, such as 'August Beauty', an upright form that flowers from May to October or November.

According to Dirr, 'First Love' (or 'Aimee Yoshida') is five feet tall and three feet wide and boasts a long flowering period. 'Fortuniana' features larger leaves than the species and flowers up to four inches wide. Cultivar 'Chuck Hayes' has semi-double white flowers in May and June and is reported to be more cold hardy than most. 'Miami Supreme' has dark-green foliage and fully double flowers.

'Variegata', the variegated form, is not supposed to be as cold tolerant as the plain green. Mine has been perfectly hardy, but has not yet grown large enough to flower.

Perhaps you don't have room for one of the large shrubs. Take heart. Many smaller forms are available. Probably the best known one, 'Radicans' (or 'Prostrata'), is often used as a low evergreen groundcover. The flowers are like those on the larger shrubs, only smaller. Some branches of the variegated form, 'Radicans Variegata', may revert to green and should be pruned off. 'Veitchii' grows two to four feet high and two feet wide and flowers profusely.

'Daisy' (or 'Kleim's Hardy') is another flower form of gardenia that has become popular. It has a single or daisy-form flower, with the same fragrance and evergreen quality. At three feet high, it is easier to use in a small garden. Monrovia Nurseries lists one named 'White Gem' that grows one to two feet high, also with single flowers.

Gardenia is usually used as a specimen shrub in the landscape. It works well in a shrub border with azaleas, camellias, and hydrangeas. Like these, gardenias like acid soil that is moist and high in organic matter. It needs good drainage, so plant it slightly higher than ground level, just like its mates in the shrub border.

Now for the bad news. Gardenias are subject to many insects, such as aphids, scale, mealybugs, whiteflies, and thrips; as well as nematodes and powdery mildew. Whiteflies usually cause the most problems, but spraying with Safer's soap works well. Be sure to cover the under side of the leaves where they hide. In twenty years, I have not had any major problems.

Site your gardenia near an entrance or along a path where it can be enjoyed by those who, like me, are crazy about its distinctive fragrance. Admittedly, there are strong opinions on both sides of that issue. My own, flesh-and-blood sister thinks they're sickeningly sweet; while my mother-in-law loves them so much she carried a whole bouquet of them at her wedding.

The Lowdown on Groundcovers

Tired of pulling and pushing that lawn mower up and down a bank or steep slope? Not only is it no fun; it can be dangerous. What about those bare areas in your garden, under that big tree where nothing will grow? In both instances, a groundcover can come to the rescue.

The possibilities are endless, depending on the look you want, and whether the site is in sun or shade. The first thing that comes to mind for a sunny spot is Asiatic jasmine (*Trachelospermum asiaticum*). With its evergreen leaves and tendency to fill in tightly, it should hold that bank in beauty all year.

For a taller, looser groundcover that blooms in early spring, try the winter jasmine (*Jasminum nudiflorum*). It grows in fountain-shaped, three- to four-foot mounds and blooms early in spring with yellow flowers. It, too, is evergreen and can live in sun or shade.

If you fancy a rose, *Rosa pimpinellifolia* has small, tightly compact leaves and small white flowers. The herb rosemary should flourish in the conditions of sun and good drainage that your bank offers. It also smells wonderful and will challenge your ingenuity in finding new culinary uses for it.

Small shrubs planted closely together work well. Two small nandina cultivars, *Nandina domestica* 'Harbor Dwarf' and *N. domestica* 'San Gabriel', will grow to six to twelve feet tall in sun or shade. 'San Gabriel' has a much finer texture than 'Harbor Dwarf' and changes from reddish when young to blue-green to a reddish purple in fall and winter. If you've grown the taller variety of nandina, you know what tough plants they are.

Two creeping junipers, *Juniperus horizontalis* 'Wiltonii' and *J. conferta* 'Silver Mist', have lovely bluish tinted foliage. Both make perfect groundcovers for sun.

I did a double take when I saw a low sprawling crape myrtle 'New Orleans'. This is certainly a novel groundcover. Former Riverbanks Botanical Garden Curator Jenks Farmer says it blooms in several different colors, but can be hard to find. Nurseries Caroliniana is the only place he knows that is growing it.

Suppose you have an area that is here in sun and there in shade. Don't despair. *Cephalotaxus harringtoniana* 'Prostrata' will do the job. It has a very nice texture reminiscent of yew, its cousin. Plants will grow together to make a lovely planting. A similar sprawling shrub, *Podocarpus lawrencei*, has a finer texture and should also grow in sun or shade, although it is newer to the trade and may be harder to find.

Vines, too, can serve as groundcover. The first to come to my mind is always ivy. There are many different cultivars with small to large leaves, and in many colors. It may take a while to get ivy established, but once it is, it will choke out most weeds. Confederate jasmine (*Trachelospermum jasminoides*) also works well as groundcover, although we usually think of growing it on arbors and trellises.

At Riverbanks, I saw a handsome wintercreeper (*Euonymus fortunei* 'Sun Spot'). It climbs a wall as well as hugs the ground. Another attractive white variegated euonymus is *E. fortunei* var. *radicans* f. *variegata*. Both of these are good for smaller areas. They may even be used in beds. I have used the second in a shade planting with ferns and hostas.

Also at Riverbanks, I saw a steep hillside planted with huge crinum lilies and all the vacant soil was covered by *Sedum acre*, "probably named that because it will cover an acre," quipped horticulturist Bill Davis. While *Sedum acre* loves the sun, it will also grow in shade, though it may not be covered with as many yellow flowers in late spring. But *Sedum lineare* 'Variegatum' does even better in shade, where its white variegation and yellow flowers fairly sparkle.

Grasses and sedges and other grass-like plants offer still another option. We are all familiar with the liriopes and mondo grass. They are certainly indispensable. But *Carex oshimensis* 'Evergold' with yellow-striped leaves will also grow in shade. So will *Carex glauca*, with fine-textured, one-foot-high, spreading bluish foliage. For a similar look in sun, try grassy-leaved sweet flag (*Acorus gramineus* 'Ogon'), which has yellow variegation and low growth habit. *Stipa tenuissima* and several types of muhly grass (*Muhlenbergia* sp.) make nice soft and unusual groundcovers. Farmer says they serve admirably to hold the soil for a couple of years, despite not being long lived.

Actually, a groundcover could be any plant that grows in your site and covers the ground. Many perennials and even annuals can be used. The perennial verbena will cover a lot of territory in sun. A cultivar called 'Texas Appleblossom' looks great.

Lenten roses (*Helleborus* sp.) make a handsome and long-lived groundcover in full shade. Other perennial possibilities for shade include pachysandra, many kinds of asarum or wild gingers, *Rohdea japonica*, holly fern, Japanese painted fern (*Athyrium niponicum* 'Pictum'), white wood aster, and Bishop's weed (*Aegopodium podagraria*). One of my favorite plants is a single variegated ardisia that has been slowly spreading in a mostly shady site.

Many annuals will cover a lot of ground quickly, as you know if you've grown any of the sweet potato vines. Purple-leaved 'Blackie' and chartreuse 'Margarita' will romp through your flower bed pulling many other colors together in a harmonious whole.

And that's the lowdown on groundcovers. With so many choices, I don't expect to see bare ground anywhere. Cover it with a plant.

Gardening above the Ground

Call this an ode to pots. Garden pots that is. One of the best things we ever did in our garden was to fill a wide set of curving steps, off the back door, with an assortment of containers.

Planted with rotating seasonal displays of colorful annuals, bulbs, perennials, herbs, and small shrubs, they provide a colorful display during nine months of the year. And, with a faucet right by the steps, watering is easy. (Containers do need water every day.)

The beauty of gardening in containers is two-fold. It solves many of the problems of growing in the ground, and it offers new gardening possibilities. Got problem soil? Too wet, too dry, too hard, or too congested by tree roots? Growing in containers allows you to grow the plants you love and grow them well. Got places where there is no soil? A patio, deck, balcony, pavement, or steps? A few containers can turn an inhospitable site into a veritable gardening paradise. Got soil pests, such as nematodes that love tomatoes, figs, boxwoods, and many other plants? A container can offer you a pest-free environment.

Almost anything can be grown in a pot, although I wouldn't try Southern magnolia! And pots are so portable. Jim Wilson, of television's "The Victory Garden," has written a whole book about landscaping with containers. He reminds us that a few well-placed pots of bright flowers can have as much impact in our gardens as a new flower border. How's that for economy?

For starters, flank the entrance to your home with matching large planted containers. In a semi-shaded setting, I have created a red-and-white theme using variegated aspidistra, asparagus fern, white plumbago, 'Little Miss Muffett' caladiums, 'Dazzler Cranberry' impatiens, and red caladiums.

This selection has all the elements of a large mixed combo — tall plants for the middle or back, cascading plants around the edge, and fillers of medium height and varied textures for the remainder. Vary the shapes of flowers and consider the colors of foliage, too, and you begin to get the idea.

Kinds of Containers. Local suppliers have everything you need to get started. Containers made of concrete, wood, terra cotta, plastic, and lightweight resin copies of stone are suitable. While terra cotta is porous and allows more air for the roots, it also dries out faster than plastic or metal. If a terra cotta pot is large enough, the size will compensate somewhat for these problems. Don't forget "found" containers, such as old cast-iron pots, chimney flues, old garden boots, olive oil cans, and large baskets lined with plastic. Almost anything that can hold soil and has drainage is fair game.

Hanging baskets and window boxes are other types of containers. Both will need to be monitored so that they don't dry out. Containers that sit in the sun can be made cooler by lining the interiors with styrofoam insulation.

Soils for Containers. Never use ordinary yard soil in a container. It's not only too heavy, but it also may bring along the weeds and nematodes you're trying to elude. Choose a high-quality soil-less mix specifically labeled for use in containers — such as Peters®, Miracle-Gro®, Scott's® Metro Mix, or Fafard®. Some companies make different mixes for different kinds of plants.

Most mixes are pH balanced and contain enough nourishment to get plants started. Many gardeners like to mix in compost, such as mushroom. This is a good practice because the compost will gradually feed the plants as they are watered. I like a ratio of one-fourth compost to three-fourths soil-less mix. You may also use slow release granules (Osmocote® or similar), as well as liquid plant food. Constant watering washes out nutrients, which must be replaced.

Watering Containers.   Instead of putting a matching saucer under an outdoor container, turn the saucer upside down to lift the pot off the ground and help drainage. Excess water may cause plant roots to rot. Some companies make cute little clay feet on which to rest your container. Bricks work well, too.

Smaller containers dry out much faster than larger ones. When it's very hot, even large containers require daily watering, but small ones may need it even more often. Water-holding crystals that swell with moisture and feed it slowly to plant roots may be mixed into the planting medium when you are potting. They can also hold too much water during a rainy spell. Don't use them in pots with more drought-tolerant plants, such as succulents.

Grouping container plants close to a water source will

make them easier to maintain. Even better, if you have a drip irrigation system, you can arrange spaghetti tubing for individual pots or set up a small sprinkler head to cover several.

Plants for Containers. For each container, choose plants that have similar growing needs. Do they all like sun or shade? Wet or dry? Are the foliage and flower textures a pleasant mixture? Do the colors complement each other as well as the surroundings?

There is almost no limit to the kinds of plants you can grow in containers. Large shrubs, clipped or unclipped, may be used in pots to frame an entrance to a house or garden. Some shrubs, such as daphne, may even be happier in a container. Perennials, annuals, and bulbs, either alone or in combination, are customary, but vines and groundcovers, vegetables, and herbs can also be used.

Mixed plantings in pots are easy to put together if you keep a few simple formulas in mind: (1) Place something tall in the center of the pot, (2) put medium-height and mounding plants around it and use trailing plants to soften the edges — I have a large concrete pot planted with a 'Perle d'Or' rose surrounded by yellow variegated ivy; it forms a focal point in the front center of a flower border — and (3) use contrasting flower shapes and colors and foliage with complementary colors and textures.

Need help planning all this in your mind's eye? Visit your local garden center and try out different plant combinations. Don't be shy about organizing trial groupings on a table or the ground. Garden center employees can often help.

On one expedition to a local garden center, I looked at purple fountain grass, a bronzy cordyline, giant green liriope, African iris, dracaena spikes, and tall perennials like the *Canna* 'Bengal Tiger' for height. Then I found flowering trailers such as verbena, calibrachoa (million bells), and ivies.

Then 'Swan River' daisy and 'Golden Anniversary' lamium caught my eye.

Ferns like Boston, mahogany, autumn, and Dallas for shade look good with bacopa, impatiens, begonias, golden creeping Jenny, 'White Nancy' lamium, and a new yellow variegated vinca.

My favorite container planting this year has been a wide, clay azalea pot, combining a golden-leaved 'Emerald Tiara' hosta, purple- and silvery-leaved 'Pewter Veil' heuchera, a variegated yellow and green ivy, and the black-leaved form of mondo grass. All of these plants are perennial, so I'm enjoying them for a second year.

This combination is a real knockout in a shade border. Notice that the impact here comes from foliage colors and textures. You can use such a container to brighten up a spot under the trees, where root competition precludes planting in the ground.

Local garden designer Ruthie Lacey is famous for her container plantings. "I even planted two for myself this year," she says, "and I've really enjoyed seeing them through my office window."

In a sunny area, she likes hot colors. A bamboo-stake tepee supports a bright-yellow black-eyed Susan vine. Around this grow a yellow-and-tangerine lantana, 'Brown's Ferry Red' verbena, 'Carpet Flame' petunias, and some hot-pink portulacas with yellow centers. Purple petunias intermix and fall over the edges.

A pot of succulents may contain sedums, echeverias, or agave. Choose one of the many sun coleuses and match the multi-colors in its foliage to single-color flowers for a can't-fail combination. Following are some other great mixtures of plants that will make a wonderful impression:

Annual combination for sun: Purple fountain grass, pink gomphrena or pentas, tricolor sweet potato vine, white heliotrope, and 'Texas Appleblossom' verbena.

Annual combination for shade: African iris for tall green foliage, white bacopa, white impatiens, and white caladiums.

Vegetable and herb combination: A cherry tomato (staked) in center, with herbs, such as parsley, dill, thyme, basil, and chives; and 'Lady in Red' salvia for color.

A patio tree rose in a pot: Small pink tree rose, dusty miller, erigeron, 'Blue Bedder' salvia, or pink million bells.

So many great choices, so little chance of seeing the same pot twice.

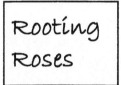

Rooting Roses

Rooting roses is my latest project. Although I love all roses, the ones that have captured my heart are the old garden roses. They are the ones our grandmothers grew, with fragrances that hang heavily in the air and in our memories. But I'm not a collector. I have a garden of many kinds of plants, the rose being just one. That's why I like roses that will grow happily with other plants. For me, putting it all together is the challenge and the fun of gardening. I also like roses that have passed the test of time and can be grown without too much fuss. I don't want to spend my Saturdays with a tank of chemicals on my back. If I grow them in a mixed border, other plants will help to camouflage any blemishes on the roses.

Any rose found growing on an old house site long after the house and its owners are gone must be one self-reliant plant. In recent years, these roses have become more available because so many rose rustlers have obtained cuttings from cemeteries, old house sites, and homes (with permission). Specialty nurseries have sprung up to grow these old roses for sale. Instead of being grafted onto the rootstock of a utilitarian variety, they are grown on their own roots.

My problem with grafted roses has been my inability to decide whether to plant them with the bud union (the grafting point) right at soil level, one to two inches above, or one to two inches below the ground. No matter what I had chosen to do, when I got out my pruning instructions in February and read, "Prune your rose back to three or four of the healthiest canes," I would usually look at my pitiful specimen and throw up my hands. How can you cut back to three or four canes when only one cane's survived? That rose bush was literally on its last leg.

The famous British gardener Gertrude Jekyll found grafted roses unsatisfactory. In her 1902 book *Roses for English Gardens*, she writes that grafted roses planted in thin soil, or well- amended and mulched soil, are unhappy by their third year. She notes that while some understock may not suit your garden, the rose grafted to it might thrive on its own roots. She suggests that grafted plants are probably best for show bloom, which requires severe pruning to produce larger blooms and shading to protect color. "[W]hereas the own root roses, bearing slightly smaller flowers — though there are exceptions even to this — fulfill their best purpose as true garden plants."

On a recent weekend in North Carolina, I took cuttings from my sister-in-law's thriving roses and plunged them in a bucket of water inside a cooler for the trip home. Then, I called my friend, rose grower Pat Henry, co-owner of Roses Unlimited in Laurens, S. C. She gave me some tips on the way to root the roses.

Pat recommends taking cuttings in the morning, while the plant is still fresh. The bush should have been well-watered the previous day. Choose a stem that is about the size of a wooden skewer, not too soft and not too hard; but just pliable enough that it doesn't break when you bend it. Make your cut about one-quarter inch below a node (the little bump on the stem where new growth starts). She then soaks the whole cutting for thirty minutes in water into which she has dissolved an aspirin.

Pat now prepares the cutting by wounding the stem opposite the eye going underground by scraping off a narrow strip of the outer layer just above the cut end. Then she cuts an "x" in the bottom of the cutting, taking care not to cut as far up as the wound. Finally, she removes the bottom pair of leaves. The cutting is now ready to be "stuck" in a soil-less mix made for starting seeds and cuttings.

One-gallon plastic nursery pots make good rooting containers. I wash my pots in a solution of one part bleach and nine parts sudsy water. After rinsing the pot, fill it with soil-less mix and water it until it is damp throughout. Dip the cut end of the rose cutting into a rooting powder like Rootone® and shake off the excess. Using a stick or pencil, make a hole about three inches deep in the soil and carefully put the cutting into it. If possible, put two nodes below the soil. Pull the soil back around the cutting and water it lightly. Professional rose growers use mist systems to keep the humidity high around their cuttings. The home gardener can cut off the bottom of a one-liter plastic soft drink bottle and place it over the cutting to create a humid environment. Remove the lid for ventilation and place the cutting in light shade.

For the first week, Pat recommends misting the leaves with water several times a day. Now you just wait, making sure the soil never dries out. Under a professional misting system, the cuttings will root in as little as three to four weeks. It may take longer for your home-grown cuttings to root, maybe two to three months. Do not disturb the plant until it has produced a firm root ball. If you take cuttings in the fall, they can be left outside over the winter by sinking the pot halfway in the ground and putting a little pine straw around it. Cuttings rooted in the spring may be ready to plant in the garden by fall,

Rose bouquet

or they can be left in their pots until next spring. Fall-rooted cuttings will be ready to plant in the garden the following fall. When the cuttings are rooted, you can begin giving them some liquid fertilizer solution at half strength.

Some roses are easier to root than others. Pat Henry says Chinas, teas, and some polyanthas are easy. Hybrid teas and old roses with lots of thorns, like the hybrid rugosas, are the most difficult. Those I've had success rooting include 'Veilchenblau' (a large shrub or climber), 'Dortmund' (a pillar rose), 'Eden' (a modern climber), 'Nastarana' (a noisette), 'Country Dancer' (a modern floribunda), 'Ivory Fashion' (a hybrid tea), and an unknown polyantha.

As you can see, any kind of rose is worth a try. And the fun of being able to exactly reproduce a rose you love at minimal cost makes the effort very rewarding. Now you may find yourself looking at roses differently. Perhaps my neighbor will give me some cuttings from that beautiful climber in her backyard.

Return of the Native

I love wildflower walks. So I reached for my Alpine wildflower guidebook when I recently packed for a trip which included a short visit to the Swiss Alps. With book in hand, every little "Ooh, look at that one!" called for a thumbing through the pages to try to identify it.

Though I didn't expect to find any overlap between the wildflowers in those Alpine mountain meadows and the wild and cultivated flowers in South Carolina, I kept seeing plants that I recognized.

Right away I noticed some of the knotgrasses, or polygonum. Many consider it a weed, and it is, albeit a pretty one. The flowers of _Polygonum bistorta_ are bright pink, and form dense, oblong clusters. A very similar form, _P. pennsylvanica_, ranges throughout much of the eastern United States. Its improved forms are available in catalogs and some nurseries.

Verbascum thapsus, which grows to four to five feet tall with woolly gray-green basil leaves and fuzzy yellow flowers in long unbranched stalks, flourishes in Alpine meadows; just as it does here in waste places. There are better forms of this biennial, and it's easy to grow from seed. One of mine, with blue-green leaves and white flowers, became more and more spectacular as it grew. The Alpine meadows hosted other smaller verbascums that also do well here.

Two surprises were hellebores and sedums. _Helleborus foetidus_, _H. niger_, and _H. viridis_ flourish in Switzerland. The most common one that we grow is the Lenten rose, _H. orientalis_, but we have the other three, also. I didn't find any hellebores in my Carolina wildflower books, so they must have been introduced here.

Sedums of many kinds grow in the rocky soil of the Alps. Among them is _Sedum acre_, a plant that happily settles in my pots, on the brick steps, or anywhere a bit of soil has washed out of a plant container.

Erigeron also attaches itself to my steps in the same way that it grows in rock crevices in Europe. I believe the one I have is *E. pulchellus*, a native to the eastern United States. Tiny daisy-like flowers with a touch of pink on the petal tips and lots of small-leaved creeping foliage make it a great filler plant for containers. I'm not sure where I got mine. It probably came as a handful of seeds from somewhere. It's a great passalong plant.

Goldenrods abound in Alpine meadows, as in our fields and along our roadsides. Among the many familiar plants I noticed were *Ajuga reptans*, forget-me-nots (Myosotis), blackberries, strawberries, Spanish broom, cherries, pears, crabapples, amelanchier, oxalis, saxifrages, sweet peas, columbine, larkspur, and the common houseleek or sempervivum. Ox-eye daisies were there in abundance, as here, but there are so many forms that I had a hard time distinguishing among them.

Plant expert Mike Creel says that more plants have been taken from this side of the Atlantic to the other, than have come our way. Often our native plants have been transported to Europe, hybridized or improved, and sold back to us. This movement of plants makes it hard for the average gardener to know what is truly native and what is introduced.

Nothing I saw made me want to come home and plant a meadow, as it is very difficult to reproduce the random beauty of plants that just happen to settle on a particular site. The commercially available "Meadow-in-a-can" may sound like a great idea, but it has been oversold to an unsuspecting public. If you do tackle this project, make sure the mix you purchase contains plants that grow in your area. The way I see it, the work of the Great Planter is a tough act to follow.

July

Grand
Old
Ladies

Crinums have been known and loved by generations of Southern gardeners. Ignored for decades, crinums are making a comeback.

Just as "rose rustlers" are rescuing old roses from cemeteries and deserted home sites, "crinum cribbers" are saving abandoned crinum bulbs from similar places. Jenks Farmer, whose car brakes for crinums, spotted a neglected crinum specimen in a disco lounge parking lot. He sent some to nurseryman Tony Avent, whose catalog now offers them under the name 'Regina's Disco Lounge'.

Crinums have common names like milk and wine lily, apostle lily, Christopher lily, Orange River lily, and candlestick lily. Despite their common names, they are actually in the amaryllis family. They produce large mounds of foliage and fragrant flowers.

True passalong plants, crinums are easy to cultivate. They can stand dry soil or places that may flood occasionally. A few will grow in water. Although they like sun, some can take the high shade found under pine trees. Full shade will produce leggy plants and few flowers. Mulch crinums with composted cow manure in the fall, and water them before and during bloom time for better growth.

While they don't divide or relocate easily, crinum bulbs (which can grow to the size of a football) are best moved in the fall by digging up the whole clump and root system, and breaking it apart. Make sure each division has a portion of the growing plate on the bottom and some roots.

Crinums are almost pest and disease free. Their durability causes Tony Avent to call them "a horticultural IRA for your grandkids." As crinum aficionado Jim Porter says, "Plant crinums in a place where you never plan to plant anything else." Use them as specimen plants, or as architectural features at each end of a border. Plant them with their long necks out of the ground.

Because crinums have been freely hybridized, there's one that's right for any situation. For small gardens, consider 'Hannibal's Dwarf'. It multiplies fast, produces abundant deep-pink flowers in midsummer, and repeats in the fall. The miniature American crinum (*C. americanum*) is only eight inches tall with wide spreading foliage that resembles a fat liriope.

Crinums

Larger varieties include long-flowering 'Ellen Bosanquet', with deep rose-red fragrant blooms, and strappy five-foot-long foliage. *Crinum x powellii* 'Album', is a superb plant with snow-white flowers; it grows in sun or part shade. The lovely pale pink flowers of *C. x powellii* 'Roseum' have a dark rose line down the center of each petal. 'Cecil Houdyshel' has rich pink flowers that bloom prolifically from May through August. 'J. C. Harvey' offers clear pink flowers, and heavily ribbed, lush foliage. 'Regina's Disco Lounge' produces a large fountain of green strap-shaped foliage and, in midsummer, flower stalks each with a dozen pink, trumpet-shaped blooms. 'Emma Jones' has deep pink, ruffled blooms and an exotic fragrance. 'Walter Flory' is only two feet tall, and its pink bicolor flowers bloom early. Also small, 'Bradley' is fragrant, with deep wine-red, white-throated flowers.

Crape
Myrtles
Signal
Midsummer

You know it must be midsummer if the crape myrtles are blooming. Nothing says summer in the South like the large colorful clusters of white, red, pink, or lavender that smother these popular trees in July and August.

Faithfully providing welcome color while the color of most trees or shrubs is on vacation, the crape myrtle doesn't limit its contribution to summer. The small crimson, orange, and yellow leaves of our neighbor's huge crape myrtle form a kaleidoscopic carpet each autumn on the brick path between our gardens. I don't have the heart to disturb this beautiful creation until the leaves have faded. Then I rake them up and toss them in the compost pile. In winter, the crape myrtle graces the landscape with an elegant sculptural effect. Gray, peeling bark on its sinewy trunks reveals handsome shades of brown, gray, and cinnamon.

Using Crape Myrtles in the Landscape. When buying a crape myrtle it is important to know which cultivar you are getting, as they come in all sizes. Some will grow to be thirty-foot trees; others will reach a modest twelve feet; and the dwarfs and miniatures might only reach a height of three to five feet at maturity. The medium (six to twelve feet) and tall (up to twenty-five or thirty feet) are the most useful in the landscape.

A tree's label should tell you its name, flower color, cold hardiness, and its eventual size. Labels merely saying "Red Crape Myrtle" will not help you site your plant properly.

Crape myrtles lend themselves to many uses in the landscape. The tallest varieties make good shade trees, providing light-dappled shade that allows other plants to grow below them. In fact, an evergreen groundcover underneath can help to set off the tree in its surroundings.

I have used a 'Byers Wonderful White' crape myrtle in a bed of ivy in our front yard. It helps to balance a lower roofline behind the tree with the higher roofline on the other end of our house front. With light and airy foliage, it still allows me to see out our windows.

If you have a small yard, there are crape myrtles that would make perfect specimen plants. For a townhouse garden, there is even a cultivar named 'Townhouse'. Small and compact, it has wine-red bark and white flowers.

Use crape myrtles in the curve of a driveway; plant a row on either side of a walk or drive to form a canopy; or make them the focal point of your patio or deck. If you are planting them as specimen trees in the lawn, they look even better if complemented with a background that will help to emphasize their flowers and form. A Southern magnolia would be perfect.

Crape Myrtle Care. Another plus for the crape myrtle is its ability to grow in a variety of soil conditions. It will grow in acidic or neutral soil. Its main requirements are sun and good drainage.

The most common problems are aphid infestation, sooty mold, and powdery mildew. Always be on the lookout for aphids, especially in the early spring. If you get them early with strong sprays of water or an insecticidal soap, the sooty mold will not have a chance to develop. You can control powdery mildew with any fungicide labeled for its treatment. Fortunately, many newer cultivars are much less susceptible to these problems.

With so many types, colors, and sizes, it is best to choose your crape myrtle when it is in bloom. If it is container grown, you can plant it now. Just remember not to let it dry out. When it becomes established (in about a year) it can tolerate periods of drought.

Don't Commit Crape Murder. And now for a few words about pruning crape myrtles. Somehow a lot of people got the idea that a crape myrtle should be cut back to around eye level every year. This results in an unsightly knot of growth that denies you enjoyment of one of the crape myrtle's prime advantages — its lovely winter tree form.

It is best used as a multiple trunk tree, with only removal of twiggy growth or too-crowded trunks (leaving three or four is good) and suckers around the plant's base. If you need a shrub form, buy one that is meant to stay shrub size. Tip pruning is all that is needed for crape myrtles. As they bloom on new wood, this can be done from late winter to early spring. During the blooming season, if you remove spent blossoms it will encourage your tree to keep blooming.

Not Just White or Watermelon Red. Crape myrtle no longer comes in just watermelon red or white. Plant breeders have been busy creating new cultivars in sizes and colors for any garden.

The common crape myrtle (*Lagerstroemia indica*) from Korea and China is cold hardy to Zone 7. A newer introduction from Japan (*Lagerstroemia fauriei*) is more cold tolerant, surviving through Zone 6. Noted for its outstanding mahogany red bark, it is also much less susceptible to fungal diseases than *L. indica*, but it blooms only in white. It makes a large tree that reaches thirty feet and more.

Plant explorer John Creech brought cuttings of *L. fauriei* to the U. S. National Arboretum in 1956. Don Egolf crossed them with *L. indica* cultivars to produce crape myrtles that have the cold hardiness and disease resistance of *L. fauriei* and the range of colors found in *L. indica*. You can recognize many of these plants by their native American names: 'Comanche', 'Muskogee', 'Seminole', 'Sioux', 'Tuskegee', and 'Tuscarora'.

One of the most popular crape myrtles is the 'Natchez' white, another National Arboretum hybrid. With larger leaves and flowers, and more disease resistance, it is a worthy specimen. It has a much denser canopy than *L. indica* varieties, making it a real shade tree at maturity (twenty feet).

Crape myrtle

Nurseryman Ted Stephens has high praise for the medium height (twelve-foot) 'Sioux': "It has one of the most enticing pink flowers ever. But the outstanding thing is its clean, disease-free foliage."

In his *Manual of Woody Landscape Plants*, Michael Dirr describes a huge number of crape myrtles, which is the basis for the following list. All are *L. indica* x *L. fauriei* introductions from the National Arboretum.

Semi-Dwarf (5 to 12 feet)

Cultivar	Flower color	Trunk color	Fall color
'Acoma'	Pure white	Light gray	Red purple
'Caddo'	Bright pink	Light cinnamon brown	Orange-red
'Hopi'	Clear light pink	Gray-brown	Orange-red
'Pecos'	Clear medium pink	Dark brown	Maroon
'Tonto'	Fuschia	Cream to taupe	Maroon
'Zuni'	Medium lavender	Light brown-gray	Dark red

Intermediate (13 to 20 feet)

Cultivar	Flower color	Trunk color	Fall color
'Apalachee'	Light lavender	Cinnamon to chestnut brown	Orange-russet
'Comanche'	Dark coral pink	Light sandalwood	Purple-red
'Lipan'	Medium lavender	Near white to beige	Orange-russet
'Osage'	Clear light pink	Chestnut beige	Red
'Sioux'	Dark pink	Medium gray-brown	Maroon to red
'Yuma'	Bicolored lavender	Light gray	Yellow-orange

Tree Type (23 to 33 feet)

Cultivar	Flower color	Trunk color	Fall color
'Biloxi'	Pale pink	Dark brown	Orange-red
'Choctaw'	Clear bright pink	Light to darker cinannon brown	Bronze-maroon
'Miami'	Deep coral pink	Dark chestnut brown	Red-orange
'Muskogee'	Light lavender	Light gray-brown	Red
'Natchez'	White	Cinnamon brown	Orange to red
'Tuscarora'	Dark coral pink	Light brown	Red-orange
'Tuskegee'	Dark pink to red	Light gray-tan	Orange-red
'Wichita'	Light magenta	Russet brown to mahogany	Russet to mahogany

Making Gardening Easier

Gardening is difficult. A *Wall Street Journal* article titled "The Lazy Gardener" noted that more than half of all gardeners are baby boomers. "They're reaching an age when spending sweaty afternoons on their knees is getting a little tougher. Younger gardeners, meanwhile, tend to be on the impatient side; the faster the plants grow, the better."

There's something about the heat of a South Carolina summer to make me wonder if there aren't easier ways to enjoy gardening.

Water. It is better to water deeply and less frequently so that your plants will develop a deep root system. A plant that is wilting from heat is not only painful to see, but also more susceptible to insects and disease than a healthy plant. Always water early in the day. Not only is it cooler for you then, early watering also allows the leaves time to dry before evening. Diseases proliferate on wet foliage. Even if you have a drip system, morning is a better time to water, especially if you use overhead sprinklers. It helps your plants make it through the heat of the day.

Don't scatter single containers all over the yard. By grouping them together near a water source, you can water them more easily. Put them in prominent places, as you'll be more likely to water them if you see them every day and can check them. This strategy of grouping containers together works especially well when you go on vacation. Locate them where they will be reached by a sprinkler system.

A great help this year has been our new irrigation system, with sprayers for grass areas and driplines in the beds. It's amazing how much better my plants are looking, and how much happier my husband is, now that he no longer has to lug hoses around or worry about figuring out how to set timers to run a Byzantine network of hoses. Our new system can be programmed to water while we're gone, so I don't spend my vacation worrying about whether my plants are surviving.

Shrubs. Plant more shrubs, especially flowering ones. Janice Beatty, a local gardener, says, "I'm putting all my money in hydrangeas and viburnums." Shrubs simply need less care. Sharon Thompson also plants shrubs, as well as tough perennials. One of her easy planting tips is sprinkling the seeds of cosmos and zinnias directly in the beds around the Fourth of July. They sprout and make sturdy plants, and can add needed fall color to your beds.

Containers. Everybody agrees that using more containers makes gardening easier. Color can be concentrated in a few areas, and pots are easy to care for, especially when grouped together for easier watering. You can even put a group of containers on drip irrigation with little spaghetti tubes in each one. Nancy Hart likes containers because "you get a bigger impact in a small area. I used to live on 40 acres and never could get a handle on the garden, which was mostly sunny. We've bought a smaller house with a smaller garden, mostly in shade."

Tools, etc. Janice Beatty says she never goes down on her knees to garden. She has a little rolling wagon with a seat on top, handles to help her get up, and pockets to carry all the tools she needs for a job. This way she doesn't waste time and energy running back and forth. A long metal handle with a claw on the end that you work from the top is a great back saver. She also suggests we should pick our seasons. "People up north don't garden when the ground is covered with snow. Why should we try to garden when it's the hottest time of the year?"

Anne Mattox has all of her garden mulched. She leaves containers in the shade when she's gone and keeps geraniums happy in the heat by sinking the plastic pot inside a stone container. The soil around the plastic pot acts as insulation.

To beat the heat during summer gardening, Nancy Hart wears a cool collar. It's a fabric tube filled with water-absorbing crystals. After soaking the collar and freezing it, she just puts it on for cool relief.

If you have no time to garden during the day and have outdoor lighting, try night gardening. It's much cooler and more pleasant, but use plenty of mosquito repellent. White, silver, and pastel gardens seem to glow at night. Scents, such as that of the wonderful angels' trumpets (*Datura* sp. or *Brugmansia* sp.), hang heavy in the evening air. Confederate jasmine is powerfully fragrant early in the season, and moonflowers come in later in the summer.

Don't plant things that need constant deadheading or pruning. For hedges use plants that look good in their natural form. Plant groundcovers in areas where grass won't grow. This cuts down on mowing time and frustration. MULCH, MULCH, MULCH to help keep down the weeds.

Gardening indeed becomes difficult, the hotter it gets. But maybe these tips will make you a more efficient and sensible gardener, and not necessarily a lazy one.

Southern-Fried Gardening

My husband and I recently returned home from visiting English gardens. As we walked through the doors of our local airport terminal, we felt gripped by a palpable glove of heat. It was something akin to opening an oven door. I wondered what my garden could look like after three weeks in such unbearable conditions. I decided that

I would be happy if there was anything still alive, even after having left my sprinkler system programmed. No wonder plants in England are so easy to grow. In spite of receiving less annual rainfall than we get, plants flourish in summer highs of 68 to 70 degrees and lows in the 50s. Sure, they do have droughts. It even gets "hot" once in a while, catching English gardeners flat-footed and making them drag out little-used hoses to water gardens that usually need no irrigation.

You must be wondering what on earth I could say about gardening in 100-degree heat. It is a challenge, I admit; but plants cost money, so it makes sense to know their needs so that you can try to supply them.

As water supplies are strained in many areas, a concept that has gained recognition is xeriscaping. In its simplest definition, it means planting the right plants in the right places, and using irrigation more efficiently. A xeriscape is not a yard that looks like a desert. There are many trees, shrubs, perennials, and annuals that can thrive with natural irrigation (rain), or a little help from you during droughts.

You can still grow your exotic and natural plants that require more water. Just place these high-water-use plants close to the house. The idea is to group plants into separate zones according to their water needs. Plants that need more water should be closest to your home, and plants that require little or no water should be farthest away. There can be several intermediate zones with different irrigation plans. Your watering system is as critical as ever, but it should be tailored to the site. Drip irrigation or soaker hoses work well for shrubs and trees. This kind of watering is best done in the evening or at night to help them get through the day. Deep and less frequent watering to the root zones will encourage a better root system.

A lawn needs either overhead or pop-up sprinklers. Watering should be done in the morning so that the water can evaporate from the leaves before night. Lawn grass is a big water user, so make your areas of lawn smaller by increasing your mulched areas. One way to do this is to make a curving island bed around several existing trees and cover the ground with pine straw or other mulch. In the grass areas you do have, mowing them at the proper height will help them survive droughts. By setting your mower blades higher, the grass will retain enough of its green to make food for itself, and the taller blades of grass will shade the roots, keeping them cooler and lessening evaporation.

A happy plant is one that is growing in well-prepared soil with plenty of compost added once or twice a year and a good layer of mulch on top, such as pine straw or ground bark. It has the proper nutrients and water at the proper time and is planted in its favorite location of sun or shade. Sounds like a tall order, but you can have a garden that is lush and full if you follow these guidelines and use the right plants. Many perennials and annuals for sale here are Southern natives or their hybrids. They are accustomed to making it in nature and should adapt well in your garden. With a little care, they will thrive.

For more on xeriscaping, call your local Agricultural Extension Service office and ask for any booklets they may have on the subject. There may be a small fee for these. I have listed a sampling of plants that can survive low watering. Now if I could just figure out how to adapt myself to surviving this heat.

Annuals

Celosia	Cosmos
Cleome	Tithonia
Portulaca	Gomphrena
Vinca	Melampodium
Narrow leaf zinnia	Pentas
(*Zinnia angustifolia*)	Sunflowers
Marigolds	Zinnia hybrids

Perennials

Black-eyed Susan	*Lantana camara*
(*Rudbeckia fulgida*)	Sedum
Artemisia	Gaillardia
Coreopsis	Purple coneflower
Daylilies	(*Echinacea purpurea*)
Santolina	Liriope
Rosemary	*Gaura lindheimeri*
Verbena	Catmint (Nepeta)
Heliotrope	Garden phlox
Dianthus	Cardoon
Yarrow	Verbascum

Shrubs

Barberry
Flowering quince
Winter honeysuckle
  (*Lonicera fragantissima*)
Butterfly bush (*Buddleia
    davidii*)
Eleagnus
Witch hazel
  (Hamamelis)
Juniper
Yucca
Indian hawthorn
  (*Rhaphiolepis indica*)

Loropetalum
Cast-iron plant
Vitex
 Rose of Sharon
  (*Hibiscus syriacus*)
Native holly (*Ilex opaca*)
Yaupon holly (*Ilex
    vomitoria*)
Nerium oleander
Nandina
Tea olive (*Osmanthus
    fragrans*)

Trees

Golden-rain tree (*Koelreuteria paniculata*)
Hackberry (*Celtis occidentalis*)
Serviceberry
Crape myrtle
Popcorn tree (*Sapium sebiferum*)
Bradford pear
Mimosa
Poplar (Populus)
Oak, some species such as red oak and live oak
Chinese elm (*Ulmus parvifolia*)
Littleleaf linden (*Tilia cordata*)
Locust (Robinia)
Zelkova serrata (after established)

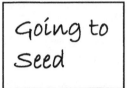

Going to Seed

Here's a way to save memories as well as dollars, and have a lot of fun in the process. At this time of year, most plants are producing seeds to carry on the species into the next season. You can gather and save these seeds and plant them next year, bringing the growth cycle full circle from seed to seed. Saving seeds is especially rewarding with annuals and many vegetables. You can even select your favorite color in a mixture of colors and save only the seeds of that flower to replant. For instance, mark with a piece of string or a twist tie, the stalks of flowers that are taller or larger or have the best color; or whatever you admire most about a plant. After the seeds mature, you can collect them from those plants only.

Most people are happy to have all the seeds they can get from plants like the peony poppy, old-fashioned cleome, larkspur, or foxgloves. While most of these will self-seed where they are growing, you might want to grow them in a different place or share some with an admiring friend. You also guarantee your supply of seed in case you don't get good self-seeding, often because of cultivation around the plant or a mulch that prevents seed contact with the soil. Poppy, larkspur, and foxglove seeds will be formed and collected in spring. To hedge your bets, you can sow some in the ground at the time they drop, just as nature would do it, and plant the rest in fall. In late summer, cleome flowers are covered with their bean-pod-like seed capsules and can be picked as they turn brown and then planted next spring.

Some plants like vinca and melampodium are going to seed themselves and come back in spite of you. No need to gather seeds from these. Just wait to see where they appear next year and transplant them to wherever you want them.

Seed-Saving Tips. I called my friend Pam Baggett, owner of Singing Springs Nursery in Hillsborough, North Carolina, for some tips on seed saving. She is an avid grower and collector of plants and a faithful participant in the seed exchange program of the Hardy Plant Society. She collects and cleans many flower seeds each year and sends them off to be distributed among members. She reminds us that seeds from hybrids do not come true. It's better to stick to the old-fashioned "unimproved" varieties.

Pam also saves seeds from tomatoes, but says the method for cleaning the seeds is a bit messy. She scoops out seed pulp from ripe fruits into a jar and allows it to ferment for a few days to kill diseases. Then she carefully cleans and dries the seeds before storing them.

You will know that seeds are ripe when the seed structure turns brown. You can hear seeds rattling around inside the pods of certain plants, indicating that they are ripe. One of these is the canna, with its prickly seedpods containing one large, round black seed. In the case of composite flowers like daisies, tithonia, or asters, the seeds are formed in the center of the flower. After the flower has turned brown and dried, you can tear apart the middle of the flower and find many dark-brown hard-coated seeds that are oblong shaped. Just think of the giant sunflower with all of its seeds in the middle to get an idea of how all the other composites work. To gather salvia seeds, pick a stalk when it turns brown, and turn it upside down inside a paper bag. When you shake it, one little black seed at the base of each bloom will fall into the bag.

Some of the seeds that Pam saves are from vines, such as the hyacinth bean vine, morning glory vines, cardinal climber, and moonflower; as well as hibiscus and grasses. If seeds are infested with bugs, she puts them on a plate and waits for the bugs to crawl away, and then dries them for a few days. Drying is very important for seeds you will be storing until next year.

Separating the Seed from the Chaff.   After gathering and drying your seeds, you must separate the seeds from the chaff. There are many methods, but I usually wind up putting them on a white paper and picking out the seeds. This is fine for a home gardener.

You can store your dried seed in a paper coin envelope, a film container, or an empty pill container, with a desiccant to keep them dry. (Save those little round desiccants that come in some pill containers.) Powdered milk can also be used as a desiccant. Store seeds in airtight containers in the refrigerator. Most will be viable for at least a year and some will last much longer. Realize that each year of storage will decrease the germination rate.

Some seeds need to be stratified, which means they need a cold spell before they are grown in a warm setting. Hellebores, which seed in spring, can be planted in pots and left outside so they can have the fluctuating temperatures they need to germinate. If you have an unusual seed that doesn't germinate after a reasonable time (a month), try placing the container inside a plastic bag in the refrigerator and giving it about six weeks of cold. Then take it out and place in a warm place again.

Some seeds, like those of goldenrod and veronica, are very tiny, almost like dust. Dry store them for six months and sow them thickly outside. Another beautiful plant whose seeds you can save is *Asarina* 'Mystic Pink', a climbing snapdragon. Its seeds look like pepper. Grasses like river oats (*Chasmanthium latifolium*) can be harvested for seed when they are completely brown in fall.

My refrigerator will soon be filled with seeds and hopes for next year. If you haven't given seed saving a try, start looking around for possibilities. Once the seed collecting bug bites you, you will see collecting opportunities everywhere.

Dreams of Monet's Garden

Sometimes dreams do come true. One of mine has long been to visit the garden of Impressionist painter Claude Monet in Giverny, some 35 miles northwest of Paris, near Vernon. A recent trip to France finally made that dream a reality. Though the mid-July morning was drizzly and cold, nothing could dampen our enthusiasm.

Monet's home itself is an integral part of the garden. It's a large, simple country house painted a soft peachy pink. The shutters and doors are a lovely, contrasting blue-green color Monet used throughout the garden because he thought it was the perfect complement for green foliage.

The place to start your visit is from the upstairs windows of the house, where you get a bird's eye view of the garden's simple layout. It is divided into two parts by a long, nasturtium-lined path through a large arbor of blue-green arches. This adds height to a flat open landscape, as do the many umbrella-like supports for pillar roses. The two halves of the garden are rectangles divided into straight rows of flowers (for picking and for painting). Outside these are square beds and greenhouses Monet built for his ever-growing collection of plants.

Hidden by trees and separated from the house garden by a road is the famous lily pond with its two Japanese bridges (painted blue-green, of course). Emerging from the tunnel under the road is like stepping into heaven. A woodland path weaves through the surrounding trees and keeps bringing you to a view of the pond from a different perspective. Each view provides another Kodak moment. Weeping willows along the banks create reflections in the placid water. Water lilies of many types and colors decorate the surface.

The larger Japanese bridge is covered with wisteria vines and creates a lovely vision.

My only frustration was waiting for the woman in the red coat, or the group of tee-shirt-clad visitors to move on. Actually, one of my favorite shots of the bridge includes a beautiful Japanese woman in a chic, beige raincoat carrying a red umbrella.

Monet created his garden to give him subjects to paint. Initially able to work it himself, he hired several gardeners as he sold more paintings. He had a passion for collecting plants of all kinds (a weakness we plant-aholic gardeners can sympathize with). "All my money goes into my garden," he said. But also, "I am in raptures."

However, Monet's greatest interest was capturing on canvas the ever-changing play of light on the water and the floating lilies. He strived to paint what he felt when he looked at the different forms of light. The large and famous paintings of water lilies were painted in his declining years. By this time, his vision had become so blurred by cataracts that he painted this dream-like series from memory.

I brought home several ideas from this garden built by a man whose passion for gardening and talent for painting were inextricably linked. Monet liked flowers planted in broad swaths of color, so color was mainly what the eye sees. Being able to view the garden from upstairs clarifies the design concept. Height can be added to an open garden space with arbors and tall supports for roses. A walk through the woods should be planned with many open spaces that each reveal a different view. But the main thing I took away from Giverny was inspiration to keep working toward my dream garden.

August

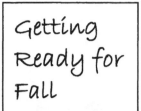

Getting Ready for Fall

If your garden is anything like mine, I'll bet it's looking pretty pooped out this time of year. But Mother Nature has help on the way, and it's not a bottle of Geritol. It's called fall.

Like a long-awaited festival, one of the year's most glorious seasons will soon be at hand. Southern gardeners eagerly anticipate the lovely cool days that make outdoor work a pleasure, not a punishment.

Things that Bloom. Many plants save their blooms for fall. Their beautiful oranges, yellows, and reds reflect the changing colors of leaves. Among many are bright-yellow cosmos, fiery orange tithonia, and the cardinal climber, which carries its tiny red tubes up arbors and fences, and rambles over shrubs.

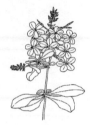

Plumbago

Flowers that accompany these bright hues are purple (Mexican salvia and *Euphorbia purpurea*), white, silver (santolina and dusty miller), blue (plumbago), as do a large number of bronze leaves (ajuga 'Mahagony', 'Burgundy Glow', and 'Chocolate Chip'). Gardener Val Hutchinson's favorite fall combo is purple Mexican sage with orange tithonia and yellow swamp sunflower.

Of course, good old reliable mums come in great fall colors ready to plop into containers. Toad lilies and fall anemones join the show. Confederate roses (actually a type of hibiscus) will add their huge blooms.

Floride McKoy's autumn clematis is blooming in her Stateburg garden. Her fragrant white ginger lilies will soon follow. Manning's Marie Land has red, orange, pink, and white ginger lilies.

Good Carry Overs. Many plants from your summer garden continue to perform and even perk up in cooler weather. Ornamental grasses have lovely blooms that will soon turn into beige for winter. Cannas still bloom in all colors, and sun coleuses have been getting larger all summer. Black elephant's ear (Colocasia) may bloom with a yellow tropical-looking flower. Buddleias continue to bloom if they are deadheaded. Remontant roses will repeat well with a bit of pruning, cleaning up, fertilizing, and watering.

Coleus

Things that Fruit. Marie Land says there's no more beautiful fruiting tree than the Oriental persimmon with its plum-sized, bright-orange fruit. Yvonne Russell loves to see the scuppernong vines (Frye and Dixieland) and muscadine vines (Black Beauty and Sugargate) bearing heavily in her garden. She suggests planting them on a post-and-wire fence or a wall rather than on arbors, as they are messy to walk under. Kiwi vines can be treated the same way. Their bare vines in winter make beautiful tracery on a wall. Beautyberry shrub has gorgeous magenta berries for fall arrangements.

Things to Plant. Seeds of biennials, such as bread poppies, larkspur, and money plant should be ordered now so that they can be planted in September or November. It's time to start the fall vegetable garden. Minnie Kelley has planted lettuce, kale, carrots, and collards in her garden. Nurseries and garden centers will have ornamental vegetables, including the 'Red Russian', 'Peacock', 'Red Ruffles', 'Red Bor', and dinosaur kales, along with 'Bright Lights' chard. Pansies and violas can be planted when it's cooler. Rebekah Kline says the Delta series is one of the best performers. The Bingo series will bloom in some shade.

It's not too late to plant colchicum bulbs and autumn crocus.

Fall Tips. Marie Land suggests cutting faded, green flower heads from hydrangeas for drying and collecting rose petals for potpourri. Also, root cuttings of azaleas and camellias; and collect seeds for next year.

Minnie Kelley records what's blooming each month; and Floride McKoy checks local nurseries for deals on spring and summer perennials and shrubs.

Fall is poised to renew our spirits, lure us into the garden after the dog days of August, and excite us about new plants, bulbs, and old favorite perennials and annuals.

Shade in the garden — a problem or an opportunity? As I've never had a really sunny garden, this is a subject I've given a lot of thought to over the years. I've been gardening in my present garden in Columbia for twenty-two years. As it's in an old downtown neighborhood with a lot of hardwood trees, I've had to learn how to cope with varying degrees of shade as well as tree roots, falling leaves, dropping limbs, acorns, nuts, and everything else that oak and pecan trees can shower upon you. I'd like to pass along to you some of the things I've learned about gardening in shade.

First of all, if you have a shady garden, count your blessings. Imagine how much those mature trees would be coveted by the owner of a new home surrounded by a sea of lawn and a few little saplings. There's no doubt that large shade trees lend a look of stability and maturity to a home. Another plus is the comfort factor of shade versus sun in our climate. Stand in the full sun on a day in midsummer. Then step into the shade of a tree and decide where *you* would rather dig and plant and pull weeds! Or where you would rather sit and read a book or eat your lunch.

We can all probably agree on the energy-saving factor of shade, but that still leaves us gardeners wondering what will grow in it and how to design a varied and colorful landscape around it. Even if you consider your garden to be mostly sunny, I'll bet that you have some shady areas that you may not have developed to their full potential.

As with any garden, a shade garden should begin with a good plan. This calls for research and observation. A good place to start learning about shade is in the woods or in a park in your locale. Go for walks at every season of the year. Take your field guide and a notebook and pen and perhaps a camera.

You've probably noticed how the plants grow in layers in a forest. Notice what plants make up those various layers. What kinds of understory trees and shrubs grow there and when do they flower? In a mature hardwood forest, much of the bloom comes in the early spring before the leaves of the tallest trees emerge. There are many perennials and bulbs that bloom during this season of sunshine. Also notice which plants grow in the middle of the woods and which choose the more open and brighter setting at the edge of the forest. Which ones grow in high and dry places and which prefer the damper stream bank?

Get down on your hands and knees and examine the soil conditions. A working knowledge of how plants grow in their native habitat is essential if you are going to try to reproduce those same conditions in your garden. Actually, most native plants in a home garden will outperform their country cousins if they are given the right light and soil conditions because they have less stress and competition. Some Queen Anne's lace that I once brought into my garden grew to be six feet tall.

In addition to the many native plants that are available from a growing number of Southern nurseries, there are many shade-loving plants from other parts of the world that you can grow, too. As long as the climate and soil conditions of their native habitat are similar to those in your garden, they should do fine and will add greatly to the interest and diversity of your shade garden. Now, you will also need to observe the patterns of shade in your own garden and try to define just what kind of shade you have so that you will know what kinds of plants should do well and in what areas. If possible, observe the different areas of your garden for a whole day during every season. Notice where the sun comes up, what time it strikes each area, and how long it lasts. Is it afternoon shade, morning shade, or all-day shade? Even all-day shade can vary according to the kind of plants overhead and the season of the year. Obviously, the most difficult location to deal with will be under evergreen trees. You may have to do a little editing in the form of selective pruning or even removal in order to open things up a bit.

Assess the condition of your soil. Have it tested by the local Agricultural Extension Service. Ask for an evaluation of the organic matter in your soil. Whether you have sand or clay, you will probably need to add organic matter to help sandy soil hold more water and nutrients and to help clay soil hold more air and drain better.

Soil preparation is critical for any kind of garden, especially for a shade garden where there is a lot of root competition from trees and shrubs. When planting under large trees, you need to know what kind of roots you are dealing with. Under deep-rooted trees, like pecans or oaks, you should be able to dig carefully around the tree and enrich the soil with several inches of compost. Plant choices here are very wide, and you can have a lot of interesting combinations. Where the roots are close to the surface, as with some of the maples, you may have to choose among some tough ground covers, such as mondo grass, holly fern or aspidistra, or perhaps some tiny bulbs. You can add a couple of inches of rich top-soil or compost over the roots of trees in order to get groundcovers started. As long as you don't add any more than that, you will not harm the tree.

Finally, remember that a garden is more than a collection of plants. Before you start planting, begin with a plan for your garden based on your own observations of the site and your family's needs and wishes. Whether it will be a mulched path cut through an existing woodland and enhanced with more native plants or a sophisticated garden of brick paths, clipped hedges, blooming evergreen shrubs, and choice perennials, careful planning will pay big dividends in enjoyment of your garden. If you are a plant nut like me, you can understand how people get so carried away with the plants they want to grow that they neglect to build the proper setting for them first.

Plant possibilities abound. For ideas on creating your own beautiful garden made in the shade, try Ken Druse's book, *The Natural Shade Garden.*

Divide To Multiply

Wouldn't you know it, even in late summer there are still garden jobs that need doing! If your daylilies or bearded iris had no blooms, your plants are probably telling you they're crowded. Generally, they need dividing every three to four years. New plants from the harvested divisions can fill an empty space in your garden, or be given to neighbors and friends.

How to do it? I asked an expert in Blythewood, Peggy Jeffcoat. She and husband Jim own Singing Oakes Garden, a certified demonstration garden of the American Hemerocallis Society.

Dividing Daylilies

1. If preparing a bed for your new plants, have the soil tested first. Daylilies like a pH from 6.5 to 6.8. Add lime only if the test results show a deficiency.

2. Your new bed needs at least six hours of sun. Prepare the bed by breaking up the soil with a shovel. Mix in one-third compost (mushroom, Black Kow®, or Earth Healer® brand), one-third aged ground pine bark, and one-third soil. Peggy adds small amounts of other amendments, such as cottonseed meal, alfalfa meal, and gypsum (usually available at your local feed and seed store).

3. Let your new bed (and your back) rest for three weeks.

4. To divide the clumps, cut the foliage back to six to eight inches, and pull off old foliage from the plant's base. Dig up the clump. Divisions can often be teased apart with your fingers. If you meet resistance, hose off the dirt to expose all the roots. Peggy uses a screwdriver to pry apart recalcitrant clumps.

5. Plant divisions in a hole prepared with a mound of soil in the center. Spread the roots out over the mound and pull soil around them. The crown (where the roots and foliage join) should be covered with no more than one inch of soil over the roots. To replant small divisions, dig three holes in a triangular formation about twelve inches apart. These will soon fill in and make a nice clump.

6. Water with a solution of Miracle-Gro® 15-20-15. Peggy notices the difference if she skips this step.

7. Keep your plants watered, but not wet.

Dividing Bearded Iris

1. Bearded iris also need six or more hours of sun. They like a pH of at least 6.8, so have your soil tested to determine if you need lime and how much.
2. Prepare the bed for iris just as you do for daylilies.
3. Iris foliage should be trimmed into a fan shape about six inches tall.
4. Clean the plants, pulling off dead foliage. Use a sharp knife to cut off parts of the rhizome that are old and soft, or rotten; as well as old, "mother" rhizomes showing no green growth. Never compost this stuff. You don't want diseased material in your pile.
5. A healthy rhizome should have green foliage and roots. Throw away small ones. They won't make good plants.
6. Cut each rhizome at the joint, and plant those with leaves in a hole with a mound of soil in the center, just like the daylilies. Space the plants about eighteen inches apart. Spread the roots over the mound and cover them with soil, leaving the rhizome exposed. Peggy says that iris rhizomes seem to like to bake in the sun.
7. Set the plants with the fan in the direction you want it to grow.
8. Do not over water iris. They like fairly dry conditions.
9. Fertilize with 5-10-5 in March, again after they bloom, and again in October when you fertilize your daffodils.

Now, go forth, divide, and multiply.

Splendor of the Grasses

Though nothing can bring back the hour
Of splendor in the grass, of glory in the
flower.

—William Wordsworth
"Ode on Intimations of Immortality"

Add the splendor of ornamental grasses to your garden. These are grasses that are neither walked upon nor mowed. Americans have become used to thinking of grass only in the context of soft turf underfoot; but the grass family contains a whole category of plants that offer beauty and color through four seasons, texture and movement in the garden, and low maintenance.

The native grasses that clothe the fields and roadsides of America are such an integral part of the landscape that they have been overlooked as potential garden plants. Ornamental grasses include these hardy natives and their improved cousins, as well as the sedges, rushes, and bamboos. Heights range from several inches up to ten-foot giants. Many have lovely blooms. Grasses ceased to appear in catalogs after the 1930s and were not used anymore except in prairie plantings until the 1970s.

Fortunately for American gardeners, the German nurseryman Karl Foerster continued to grow and experiment with ornamental grasses long after the 1930s. Thanks to his influence, and the efforts of nurseryman Kurt Bluemel and the design team of Wolfgang Oehme and James van Sweden, there is tremendous interest in ornamental grasses for public and private gardens.

Why should you grow these ornamental grasses? Because of their beauty, adaptability, variety, and ease of maintenance. Just as the native roadside grasses provide a constant background for an ever-changing display of wildflowers, cultivated grasses can perform a similar service in the home garden. They look equally at home in naturalistic plantings, where they give an informal sense of the country, and in more formal garden settings, such as mixed borders of shrubs, roses, perennials, and annuals.

At Riverbanks Zoo, grasses perform in the spotlight and behind the scenes. A sea of fountain grass (*Pennisetum alopecuroides*) backed by tall and stately clumps of ravenna grass (*Erianthus ravennae*) frames the entrance, evoking the feel of an African plain. At the edge of the new water garden, the slender, silver-touched blades of *Miscanthus sinensis* 'Morning Light', a three- to four-foot medium-height grass, blend effectively with perennials. Grasses such as *Miscanthus sinensis* 'Silberfeder' will also be used extensively in the zoo's African savannah, according to Jim Martin, former curator of horticulture.

Jim offers several tips on culture. Grasses are fairly low-maintenance plants, but like perennials, they respond best to being placed in well-prepared soil. At the zoo, that means adding lots of compost. He may fertilize once a year with 10-10-10. He cautions that new orders will be shipped from mail-order sources rather late in the spring, and should be kept well-watered until they are established. You will probably want to cut back last year's foliage around the first week of February. Most grasses do not need dividing very often, but when they do, it should be done only in the spring, just after the new growth can be seen emerging. Use two garden forks back-to-back to pry the clumps apart into two or more new clumps, and replant. Some of the large grasses may require a pruning saw.

According to Jim, "Ornamental grasses should be a staple in the garden, adding bulk and structure much like a shrub. It is a good transition plant, carrying the garden through four seasons of interest." Grasses provide a burst of green growth in the spring, fullness in the summer border, colorful inflorescences when little else is in bloom, movement and sound as they are caught by the wind, and color and interest through the winter.

Needing little extra water, no spraying for pests and diseases, and little fertilizer, ornamental grasses are much friendlier to the environment than their demanding turf grass cousins. Because they never need stalking, deadheading, or pruning, except once in the early spring, they are also low maintenance. There are grasses available for the home garden that fit into any condition of sun or shade, wet or dry soil. It is easy to be captivated by such versatile plants. Many, like miscanthus, are best used as feature plants. Others, like pennisetum, can be massed as ground cover. Calamagrostis offers a good vertical line. There are so many good cultivars it is hard to mention only a few.

To learn more about how to grow and use ornamental grasses, look for Carole Ottesen's book *Ornamental Grasses: The Amber Wave* and another by Thomas A. Reinhardt, et al., *Ornamental Grass Gardening: Design Ideas, Functions and Effects.*

Survival of the Fittest

Here we are again at that telling time of year when it becomes evident which plants had the right stuff. How many of those fresh, promising, springtime plants expired in the summer's heat and drought? And which could be candidates for the gardening version of the television show "Survivor"?

Grab a pad and pencil and make a critical tour of your garden. A plant that's survived is worth using again next year and deserves the Darwinian medal for fitness.

My own garden inspection revealed a few winners. The yellow flowering shrub *Cestrum parqui* hasn't skipped a beat. It grew to six feet after being cut to a foot above ground in early spring. Another success is my windmill palm.

Sun coleuses did the best for me, as it did for many other gardeners. Coleuses are readily available in colors to combine with any flowers. A scrumptious coleus called 'Aurora' looks stunning with purple fountain grass. It features deep pink stems and large, mostly white leaves flushed with pink.

Calls to other Master Gardeners produced a surprising number of plants that survived and even flourished. Janet Smith says her *Daphne odora* has never looked better, and her Confederate rose is also doing well.

Margot Rochester's long list of success stories includes sweet autumn clematis and Becky's daisy, which she reports "just kept going all summer." *Salvia guaranitica* has been a butterfly and hummingbird magnet for her; as have buddleia, rose pink gomphrena, cuphea, and a plant called dicliptera with gray foliage and orange flowers. She got a third bloom from her crape myrtles by keeping the seedpods cut off.

"We dug a new well," says Janice Beatty, "and we've really been watering a lot. 'Cabaret' miscanthus grass looks fabulous, but I can't understand why one of the two hyacinth bean vines I planted on each side of my steps has gone crazy and the other is doing nothing." She vows never to plant another bacopa, but will definitely repeat a successful combination of 'Lemon Drop' lantana and Purple Heart vine.

Cindy Lee says she thinks "they're going to have to rewrite some of the books recommending full sun for many plants. It's often just too much in our climate." Her plants that did survive "if you water them" include phlox, verbena, veronica, all the salvias, coneflowers, cannas, and most vines. Ornamental grasses blooming now make a beautiful addition to the border. Annuals that thrived are melampodium, scaevola, sweet potato vine, and flowering vinca. Cindy's hardy shrubs include barberry, nandina, pomegranate, blue-

berry, abelia, wax myrtle, tea olive, Indian hawthorn, oleander, gardenia, and holly.

Sharon Thompson's big bed has thrived with only weekly
attention. The secret is very good soil preparation. She's been
happy with burgundy castor bean, sun coleus, big zinnias
(probably because of no water splashes), 'Powis Castle' artemisia, and old-timey four o'clocks. "Once you have these,
you have them forever." A well-behaved goldenrod (*Solidago
rugosa* 'Fireworks') serves quietly as a "tidy backbone" for
her flower bed from spring to frost. In autumn it explodes
into arching yellow panicles.

Hydrangea

"I'm loving hydrangeas more
and more," reports Martha Wilkes
from Winnsboro, "even though I
do have to water them. My hostas
look pretty good, maybe because
it was too dry for slugs." She says
Winnsboro deserves the title "The
Lantana City" because so many
people copied the successful planting around the town clock.

A civic planting in Columbia
around the Gonzales obelisk at the
corner of Senate and Sumter
Streets survived handsomely. Its white *Zinnia linearis*, multi-
color lantana, and blue salvia combine wonderfully with pink
fairy rose.

Got plants that have thrived? Enter them in the state fair
flower show, and maybe yours will be the "survivor" in its
category.

A South Carolina Treasure

As a garden writer, I was blessed with the opportunity to visit two extraordinary gardens. One near, one far; both inspired by art.

Claude Monet's garden in Giverny, France, was a setting for many of his paintings. Brookgreen Gardens, between Pawleys Island and Murrell's Inlet, South Carolina, features the works of Anna Hyatt Huntington, one of America's preeminent outdoor sculptors. Huntington and her husband, Archer, bought four abandoned rice plantations; and, in 1931, founded our nation's first public sculpture garden. More than five hundred works by more than two hundred artists make it America's largest permanent outdoor display of figurative sculpture.

A visit to Brookgreen really begins at the front gate, where Anna Huntington's massive sculpture of two horses in fighting stance piques your curiosity about what lies inside.

Go first to the visitor's center to view the ten-minute movie, *Gray Oaks of Mystery*, for an appreciation of the garden's history. Then head for the entrance to the garden where Anna Huntington's graceful *Diana of the Chase* occupies the center of a large pool. There are approximately ten garden "rooms." The White Garden beyond, planted with white gomphrena, hybrid lilies, ginger lilies, white salvia, and chartreuse sweet potato vine, is a perfect complement for the pool's dark water.

Straight ahead is the Oak Allee Garden, a large rectangle formed by a pierced serpentine brick wall. Experience the tranquility of strolling under 225-year-old live oaks, draped in Spanish moss and resurrection fern. Then stroll around the paths adjacent to the wall, where colorful raised beds of seasonal plantings fill the spaces formed by the curving wall.

Read the touching inscriptions of poetry by many different poets, including Archer Huntington, spaced at regular intervals on the walls. From this central garden, curving paths designed in the shape of a butterfly form many more garden rooms to showcase the sculpture collection.

The Garden Room for Children will delight you and your youngsters with its animal sculptures, pool and fountain, vine-covered hut made of old oak limbs, butterfly garden, and Bear's Den. Several other theme gardens were designed with children in mind.

The largest sculpture in the garden is *Pegasus*, which requires a whole green field to contain its commanding white presence. Smaller sculptures by famous artists, such as Frederic Remington, are housed in the Rainey Sculpture Pavilion.

Brookgreen is home to more than 2,000 species of plants. Every season of the year has its own features. Spring brings a magical display of azaleas, dogwoods, and bulbs. Fall features thousands of mums. Mild winters offer their own delights. Imaginatively planted containers and beds are a summer highlight. There are many ideas for your own garden. Brookgreen's horticulturist says that he tries to use plants that visitors should be able to find in their local garden centers.

Pontoon boat rides take you into the tidal marshes and old rice fields. As Brookgreen is a nature sanctuary, expect to see wildlife, from alligators to bald eagles, along its three wildlife trails.

Visit Brookgreen in any season. Truly a South Carolina treasure, this perfect combination of art and gardening was left by the Huntingtons for all to enjoy. A poem by Pearl Council Hiatt at the entrance concludes: "There where the ancient trees wait, hushed and dim. May you find God, and walk awhile with Him."

September

The White Fringe Tree and the Star Magnolia

Just when you thought it was time to put away those garden tools, here I am to tell you that a very important season for your garden is at hand. Along with raking, composting, mulching, ordering and planting spring bulbs, and collecting and storing seeds of favorite plants, it's also the perfect time to add a flowering tree or two to your garden. Why now? Because a container-grown or balled-and-burlapped tree will need time to settle into its new home and begin growing the strong roots needed to support those pretty spring flowers you so cherish. If you plant it in the spring, it will struggle to support root growth and flowers simultaneously.

White Fringe Tree. *Chionanthus virginicus* is known by several common names, including white fringe tree, Grancy gray-beard, and old man's beard. A large shrub or small tree whose shape is quite variable, it may grow wider than its twelve- to twenty-foot height. The plant is dioecious (needs male and female trees to produce fruit). Its late spring bloom consists of white, slightly fragrant flowers with strap-shaped petals borne in six- to eight-inch-long, wide, fleecy panicles on the previous season's wood. The fruit is a one-half- to one-and-one-half inch-long, blue egg-shaped drupe that makes a show in late summer and early fall, unless the birds get there first. Birds love it and will be attracted to your garden. It can adapt to sun or part shade. In the wild, it occurs along stream banks or swamp edges. No pruning is needed.

Chionanthus has no serious diseases. Famous plantsman and author Michael Dirr believes it could replace the dogwood in the popularity lists, carrying itself with "such refinement, dignity, and class when in flower." Pollution tolerant, it thrives in cities.

Another form of chionanthus is the Chinese fringe tree (*C. retusus*), which may be even more beautiful in bloom because it carries its flowers at the end of the stems. It tolerates Southern summer heat, and its dark-green leaves can turn bright yellow in the fall.

Star Magnolia. My garden is too small for the magnificent *Magnolia grandiflora*, so closely identified with Southern gardens. But the magnolias are a big family. I know that spring can't be far away when my star magnolia (*M. stellata*) opens the fuzzy gray buds that have reminded me of pussy willow all winter. The flowers of star magnolia are formed from a group of strap-shaped petals that do indeed suggest a star. One of the earliest of the deciduous magnolias to bloom, its white flowers are susceptible to freezing. Should that happen, more flowers usually follow, as they conveniently don't open all at once.

The star magnolia has a heavenly scent that beckons each time I go outdoors. Its sweet fragrance has a touch of citrus. Leaves come out after the flowers and maintain their grassy green color all summer. Although it lacks outstanding fall color, its leaves often turn almost bright yellow. Not a big tree or a fast-growing one, it's well suited for the small garden. It is multi-trunked and will have a nice small tree shape if bottom limbs and suckers are removed. 'Royal Star' is the better known cultivar, but 'Rosea' has pink flower buds opening into pink flowers that change to white at maturity.

Site your star magnolia in full sun for best flowering. Do not give it a southern exposure, lest it bloom even earlier and suffer frostbite. It prefers a peaty, organic-based soil and is very tolerant of summer heat.

Take a Fancy to Ferns

They almost escape our consciousness because they blend so well into their surroundings. But imagine standing in your garden, and closing your eyes. When you open them, your ferns are gone. In my garden, there would be gaping holes in some of my plantings and bare pockets in other places. Walking around my garden, I was surprised to count fourteen different kinds of ferns. Several of them appeared in more than one setting. How can a plant with so many uses, which is so beautiful in its own right, be almost forgotten in many garden plans?

Perhaps ferns are doing their jobs too well. They are the unsung heroes, the workhorses of the shade garden, seamlessly knitting the plantings together. There are fern societies and fern collectors, but you are much more likely to be invited to see someone's roses, perennials, or vegetables than their ferns. Well, fern appreciation is long overdue. It's time for them to stand up and toot their horns. They've been on the back row long enough.

In the middle of the nineteenth century, the British became interested in growing their native ferns indoors in terrariums and outdoors in their gardens. They formed societies that would spend Sunday afternoons digging up ferns in the countryside. Nurseries specializing in ferns offered many different varieties (usually dug from the wild).

At the beginning of this century, Boston ferns came into popularity as house plants in America. It was much later that we began growing ferns outside in the garden. In the 1950s and 1960s, a few pioneers wrote books and started societies to exchange fern spores (or seeds, in fern language). Two women in the Pacific Northwest started mail-order fern nurseries, greatly adding to the number of ferns available

and increasing public awareness. Today more and more nurseries are
propagating ferns from spores. At least
200 varieties are for sale, so there is no
reason to dig them in the wild.

One of the most useful ferns in my
garden is the holly fern, which grows
to prodigious size and remains green
all year. Visitors often ask what it is,
though it is readily available in most

Fern

garden centers. I use it in the shade with hostas, aspidistra,
woodland wildflowers, and other ferns. The East Indian holly
fern is much smaller and not as common. It has a yellow
stripe down the center of the stem (rachis). I have it in a
container with a yellow variegated and yellow flowered
lysimachia, which trails over the side.

Another container holds asparagus fern in combination
with variegated aspidistra, impatiens, and caladiums. This
fern is almost evergreen, but even if killed to the ground it
will come back from its tuber-like root stocks.

Along a shady path, I grow more ferns. Small and dainty
with glossy leaves, the Korean rock fern is usually grown as
a greenhouse plant, but it does well outside. Christmas fern
is another evergreen. A native fern, it stands out as one of
the few greens in the bare winter woodlands. The Southern
wood fern or maiden fern has fronds two to four feet long
and is easy to grow. Another native, the elegant cinnamon
fern, is even larger. It dies down in the winter and comes
back in the spring, sporting bright cinnamon-colored fertile
fronds.

A new fern in my garden is the white-back fern with
unusual star-shaped, white-backed, crinkled leaves. It likes
partial shade and well-drained soil and grows well in a rock
garden or a crevice in a wall.

Autumn fern works hard for me. It is almost as large as the holly fern but looks entirely different. Also an evergreen, it grows in shade and has beautiful coppery-pink new fronds in the spring that gradually turn to deep green in summer. The autumn fern looks great with plants that have pink flowers, like 'Pink Shades' pansies or pink impatiens. The combination of autumn fern and 'Frances Williams' hosta makes a lovely planting under my cherry tree.

The Japanese painted fern does catch your eye in a shady grouping. Not very large, its leaves of silver and blue-green make it a standout. It can also be used to good advantage in container plantings, where it makes a nice foil for flowering plants.

Several fern allies fit right in with their cousins. The arborvitae fern is really a lacy spikemoss with leaves that closely resemble the arborvitae, an evergreen conifer. It grows from creeping rhizomes that send up frond-like stems to twenty inches tall. The selaginellas are beautiful little plants that look like a cross between a moss and a fern. There are many different kinds, but only a few are hardy in North America.

Ferns naturally reproduce from spores, which appear on the backs of most fern fronds. It looks like the plant is infested with some kind of bug until closer inspection reveals a pattern too regular to have been produced by insects. While fern fanatics may enjoy collecting and planting spores, it is far easier to propagate ferns by division. Rhizomes can be divided and some species will root from a branchlet. Other ferns grow from crowns and may branch to form small plants around the parents. Separate these from the parent plant by cutting them off. Make sure that you get a sliver of parent plant and some roots. Then replant.

Provide a top-dressing of compost and water during dry spells. Most ferns like shade and rich, woodsy, well-drained soil, although a few will grow in sun. Which brings me to the sweet little ebony spleenwort, also a fern ally. I tried, to no avail, to grow it in shady, moist soil. Then one day it appeared in a chink in the mortar four feet up my brick wall. In this fairly sunny location, it has produced one offspring. How it got there remains a mystery, but it literally seems to have found its niche in my garden.

The next time you shop for plants, don't forget ferns. If you would like to learn more about these fascinating plants, I highly recommend the book, *Ferns for American Gardens*, by John Mickel.

Often Overlooked Deciduous Shrubs

When I say "flowering shrub," what do you think? If only "camellia, azalea, gardenia," come to mind, are you in for a pleasant surprise! In addition to all the evergreen flowering shrubs we are so fortunate to have in the South, there are scores of beautiful deciduous shrubs we often ignore. A plant doesn't have to be evergreen to make a significant contribution to a garden. It's nice to have colorful leaves or fruit in fall, interesting bark or bare form in winter, all in addition to the flowers we love in spring or summer. This is a reminder to those of you who are stuck on evergreen to pay attention to other kinds of shrubs.

Consider, for instance, the oak leaf hydrangea (*Hydrangea quercifolia*) with its sumptuous panicles of white flowers in spring. It holds on to these for a very long time as they gradually turn pinkish-green and finally a dry buff color. In fall the leaves are a blaze of red, orange, and green. And even disrobed in winter, its bare twisting branches and peeling bark make this a shrub that keeps on giving to your landscape.

The double-file viburnum (*Viburnum plicatum* f. *tomentosum*) is another multi-season deciduous shrub. Its white dogwood-like summer flowers are showcased against green leaves. It, too, has outstanding fall leaf color and an interesting bare winter form. Many other viburnums offer flowers or fragrance. *Viburnum carlesii* and any of its hybrids smell so sweet you will be following your nose around the neighborhood to find them.

But there are other deciduous shrubs whose flowers are so beautiful and generous, if only for a short time, that I would grow them for their flowers alone. After flowering has finished, these shrubs just fade into the green background and give structure and density to the summer garden. Mock orange (*Philadelphus coronarius*) is one such shrub. Although its season is brief, the fragrant white blossoms come at a time when spring flowers are finishing and summer flowers have not yet begun. There are many cultivars with larger, more fragrant blossoms than the species. My 'Natchez' is one of those. Its large, flat, white flowers fill the garden with their color and fragrance for two weeks. Then I usually cut it back to keep it in bounds and let it fade into the back of my border.

Kerria japonica, sometimes called Easter rose, blooms at about the same time as the Japanese wisteria. Its bright yellow little pompon blooms cover the shrub. For the discerning gardener, there are other desirable forms: a single-flowered one with paler yellow blooms and even a green-and-white variegated form that is one of my favorites. In winter this shrub loses its leaves, but the stems retain their bright-green color, adding interest for another season.

I love the flowering quince but hate the way I so often see these old-timey shrubs butchered when they are pruned. It is one of those shrubs that needs the old stems removed right to the ground each year after bloom and the others cut back at different lengths to maintain a nice, soft, rounded shape, rather than a thick cluster of stiff stems whacked off at the top. I have also seen it pruned into a green meatball shape, but the shrub that suffers most from this mistreatment is the bright yellow forsythia. It wants to be a large, loose fountain-shaped shrub, great for banks or as specimen garden plants.

All of the deciduous shrubs that bloom in spring should not be pruned until after they have bloomed, lest you lose this year's flowers. Shrubs that bloom in the summer or fall should be pruned in the early spring because they bloom on this year's new growth. The flowering lespedeza (*Lespedeza thunbergii*) that becomes a fountain of pink or white flowers in late summer should be cut right to the ground in early spring. A bonus for this plant, whose blooms the bees adore, is its vibrant orange-red fall color.

Spireas are another favorite deciduous shrub. There are several species of this old- fashioned shrub from which to choose. The earliest to bloom is the Thunberg spirea (*Spiraea thunbergii*) with white flowers in threes to fives that look like tiny umbrellas attached to the stems. It has a light and airy appearance because of its tiny leaves and its light green color. It must be pruned annually to maintain its attractiveness. *Spiraea cantoniensis*, or Reeves spirea, which is my favorite, blooms next with white flat-topped flower clusters and blue-green foliage. Its bloom may overlap that of the *Spiraea* x *vanhouttei*, a large shrub with many small white flowers. It has an arching fountain-like habit that must be maintained by proper pruning.

Other large but beautiful flowering shrubs that need the security of a large mixed border when they are not in bloom are the weigelas, which have been extensively hybridized and come in colors ranging from white to pink to red. The large form of deutzia (*Deutzia scabra*) is rarely seen, but to me is the best of the white flowering shrubs in this category. Although I have never grown beautybush (*Kolkwitzia amabilis*), it is heavenly in flower. It's listed to Zone 8, but the British seem to grow it much more than we do. I have seen it in local nurseries from time to time.

In summer there are many forms of hydrangeas to entice you, my favorite being the variegated 'Mariesii' with its blue lace-capped flowers.

Summersweet (*Clethra alnifolia*) likes a damp spot to grow and produce its small sweet-smelling pink or white flowers from July into August. There's even a form of native azalea (*Rhododendron prunifolium*) which has red flowers in July, although my soil is too dry for it. Many of these shrubs are good butterfly and bee plants. If your garden is mostly evergreen, why not make this the year to add some of these or other deciduous flowering shrubs? Don't be seduced into buying half a dozen more azaleas when they are all in bloom. Remember, most of them last for only one or two weeks, too.

Variegated Plants Add Variety

Are you afraid of variegation in the garden? According to *The New RHS Dictionary of Gardening*, "Variegation is the occurrence of patterns in the leaves of plants, due especially to differences in amounts or composition of the green pigment chlorophyll ... in a wide variety of multicoloured leaf patterns." Some gardeners are a bit leery of using variegated plants in their gardens, especially two together, for fear of making the garden look too busy. But variegated plants can add punch to an ordinary planting.

I am probably guilty of using too many variegated plants,

but I can't resist them. When I visit a nursery or garden center, it's usually a variegated plant that catches my eye. That eye-catching quality is exactly what makes them so useful in the garden, especially in the shade.

A shady border can be lit up with the addition of white or yellow variegated plants. Here, where there is not as much bloom for interest, the foliage becomes more important. Leaves marked or outlined with white look cool and refreshing on a hot summer day, while yellow variegation seems to bring a touch of sunshine into the shade.

A hosta that is variegated with white can be combined with a plant that has white flowers, such as flowering tobacco (*Nicotiana langsdorffii*), white impatiens, or white begonias. The white in the hosta leaves is repeated in the white of the flowers. This is a technique that can be used in many other interesting combinations. In the sun, a variegated miscanthus grass, such as 'Morning Light', with narrow blades traced with white, looks great with a white buddleia and white 'May Queen' daisies.

Repeating a color from one plant in another plant helps knit the border together. Garden writer Pamela Harper calls such combinations "echoes." In her very useful book, *Color Echoes: Harmonizing Color in the Garden*, she writes, "The very best echo plants are those with variegated foliage."

Although white and yellow are the most common colors in variegated plants, there are others. 'Rose Glow' barberry has smoky purple leaves mottled with pink. In our neighborhood park, we have this barberry backed by the pink climbing rose 'Eden'. Other mates are 'Anthony Waterer' spirea with round, pink, flat-topped clusters of flowers, pink coneflowers, and the small, airy, pink and white flowers of *Gaura lindheimeri*. When these bloom together in spring it is a glorious sight. Notice that here the pink variegation was echoed in three other plants, all with contrasting flower forms.

Another possibility for sun is the yellow-striped miscanthus with yellow floribunda roses, like 'Sun Flare'. In spring you could plant white tulips to come up through the green-and-white foliage of *Lamium maculatum* 'White Nancy'. And in a bed of summer annuals, try combining the pink, green, and white variegated sweet potato vine with pink zinnias, pink petunias, and/or pink cleome.

Now that we've seen how to combine one variegated plant with a plant that has solid-colored flowers, let's put two variegated plants together. Is this getting scary yet? It's easy, though, if you remember that two yellow variegated plants can harmonize if something about them is different in size or pattern or variegation. One example that comes to mind is the yellow-splashed aucuba underplanted with a hosta whose leaves are outlined in yellow.

Leaves are not the only plant parts that come in variegated form. Think about bicolored daylilies, pansies with faces, and German iris with beards in a contrasting color. One or more of their colors can be echoed in other plants. The planting possibilities begin to multiply. Soon you will feel like a conductor orchestrating a symphony.

It's easy and fun to use variegated plants in your garden if you remember a few simple guidelines:

1. Match the color of variegation in one plant with the same color in another plant of solid color.
2. Use white or yellow variegated plants to brighten up the shade.
3. Combine two plants that have the same color of variegation but different patterns or sizes.
4. Use a variegated plant anytime as an interesting backdrop for a large number of flowers of one color.

The number of variegated plants is almost unlimited, but here are some you might recognize and others you might want to look for:

Shrubs:

'Silver King' euonymus (green, white)
Barberry 'Rose Glow' (purple, pink)
Yucca 'Gold Sword' (green, yellow stripes)
Variegated weigela (green, white)
Variegated pittosporum (green, white)
Variegated boxwood (green, white, or cream)
Variegated daphne (green, white, or cream)
Forsythia 'James Mason' (green/chartreuse)

Perennials:

Variegated Siberian iris (white, green)
Liriope 'Silver Dragon' (white, green)
Ajuga reptans 'Burgundy Glow' (green, burgundy, pink)
Phlox 'Norah Leigh' (green, white)
Hosta, many cultivars and color combinations
Ligularia tussilaginea 'Aureomaculatum' (leopard plant) (green, yellow spots)
Pulmonaria (lungwort, many cultivars) (white, green)
Japanese painted fern (gray-green, silver, purple)
Lamium maculatum 'White Nancy' (green, white)
Canna 'Phaison' and 'Pretoria' (purple, red and green, yellow)
Variegated aspidistra (green, white)

Annuals:

Tricolor sage (pink, green, white)
Coleuses (many colors)
Caladium bulbs (many colors)
Pansies (many colors)
Variegated sweet potato vine (pink, green, white)
Ornamental cabbages and kales

Grasses:

Miscanthus sinensis 'Strictus' (green, yellow)
Miscanthus sin. 'Zebrinus' (green, yellow)
Miscanthus sin. 'Variegatus' (green, white)
Miscanthus sin. 'Morning Light' (green, white)
Phalaris arundinacea var. *picta* (green, white)

Get in League with Ivy

Ivy is so common that we hardly notice it. But it has many uses and comes in some 400 varieties, offering different leaf shapes and colors.

This all-purpose woody vine can serve horizontally as a groundcover or vertically as a green fence, disguising unattractive structures. With its holdfasts, often mistaken for roots, ivy easily climbs walls.

Homeowners often worry that ivy might damage the structure of masonry or brick walls. This is a myth, except perhaps in the case of extremely old walls made with a lime and sand mortar that has begun to crumble. Rather than harming brickwork, ivy can actually keep it dry and warm. In Germany, homeowners are encouraged to grow ivy on their brick houses to insulate them from frost, cold, and rain. Just keep any ivy from getting under your home's roofing material and away from painted trim.

Another myth holds that ivy kills trees. A tree covered by ivy is almost always a tree that was already diseased or damaged. Ivy is not a parasite. While it derives no nourishment from the tree, its roots do compete with the tree's roots.

When ivy is old, it produces mature growth that flowers and produces berries. The leaves will take an entirely different shape from its immature form. A dead white oak blanketed with this mature growth ivy recently toppled to the ground in my North Carolina brother-in-law's front yard. Birds, squirrels, bees, and even a litter of kittens had previously found shelter in the ivy's lush foliage. We took cuttings in hopes of rooting it, but that seems to be a job better left to an experienced nurseryman. In contrast, immature ivy is very easy to root.

I recently stopped at the gardening symposium booth of a vendor offering shrubs propagated from mature growth ivy. Despite the high prices, this "vintage" ivy was popular.

Ivy isn't particular about its soil, but it doesn't like wet feet. It can be used as a specimen plant, in a border or container, and can make a fine groundcover in partial shade. Keep it pruned to a height of two to three inches. Spring bulbs can be mixed in.

Ivy topiaries are handsome and fun to create. Jim Porter has one with cascades of beautiful ivy falling from the top of a stem he tied up and allowed to grow thick. Many smaller varieties of ivy look great in containers, perhaps underplanting perennials; and they make good houseplants.

The most common form of ivy is English ivy (*Hedera helix*). 'Glacier' is a medium-sized ivy with silver-gray variegations and white margins. 'Gold Heart' has small green leaves with a central splash of bright yellow. The leaves of 'Triton' have three points and small white prominent veins. I like the look of 'Dragon's Claw' with its curling leaves. 'Fluffy Ruffles' is even more ruffled on the edges, while 'Midget' is, as you might guess, tiny. Persian ivy (*Hedera colchica*) has leaves as big as a man's hand.

You can usually buy unusual ivies at nurseries and garden centers. Even grocery stores often sell little pots of ivy. All are hardy and can be planted outside. Several catalog nurseries also offer ivy. Ivy is the common plant with uncommonly good uses and varieties.

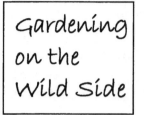

Gardening on the Wild Side

Sometimes living on the wild side can be not only exciting but also very rewarding. The wild side I mean is your garden, if you transform it into a haven for wildlife. The excitement is the hours of fun watching the grand cycle of nature. The reward is knowing that you've helped the environment at the same time.

Are we talking wild and woolly here? Are the neighbors going to raise an eyebrow or two? Says Master Gardener Val Hutchinson, "The neighborhood children, who saw what was happening in my yard, went home asking to create a wildlife habitat in their own backyards." They wanted birdfeeders and bat houses and pools, too.

Val used to be afraid of spiders. Then one day she began watching one that had made a home on her porch. "I saw how the spider caught insects and then became food for birds itself. That was about five years ago. Then I could count seven different species of birds in my garden. Now I have as many as 46, some migratory, many hummingbirds, different kinds of bees and butterflies, plus a lot of earthworms in my soil," she reports.

Just five years ago, Val became interested in having her yard certified as a Backyard Wildlife Habitat. This program, sponsored by the National Wildlife Federation, has enrolled thousands of sites, from small city balconies to hundred-acre industrial sites, since its inception in 1973.

Becoming certified is easy if you can provide four essential things for wildlife: water, food, shelter, and a safe place to raise their young.

Val began by allowing a small back corner of her half-acre lot to revert to its wild state, just to see what would appear. She also stopped using any pesticides and most commercial fertilizers. Soon her new garden contained magnolias, wax myrtle, eastern red cedar, blackberry, dogwood, and a passionflower vine. Then she added a few evergreen shrubs on her own for more color and cover in winter. She put a path through it and an old swing inside, and this has now become her favorite part of her garden.

The backyard contains several sources of water, including a pond with a waterfall, a gurgling fountain, and a bird-bath. Several attractive arbors support vines and help to add structure to the garden in winter. After putting in the pond, she found snails, then dragonfly nymphs. She added one goldfish and kept adding more until she had 36. Then a green-backed heron came and ate almost all of the goldfish. Yes, it's a jungle out there; but nature is so fascinating to watch as we safely view it from our perch atop the food chain.

Next, she moved to her sunny front yard. Here, she planted a butterfly- and hummingbird-friendly garden of flowers and shrubs, which extends right up to her mailbox. It makes one of the prettiest mailbox gardens I have seen. The sign designating her yard as a certified wildlife habitat is right there under the mailbox. A sculpture of a girl holding a butterfly net conveys to passersby the spirit of this garden. In creating it, Val has reduced the amount of turfgrass she has to water, feed, and mow, as well as the maintenance time. She also gets to watch caterpillars turn into butterflies.

If you want to create such a habitat, here's how. Plant shrubs, trees, perennials, and annuals that provide **FOOD**, such as nuts, berries, nectar, and pollen, for various creatures. Many of these plants should be native plants. Add a pond, birdbath, or just a small shallow water dish to provide **WATER** for drinking and bathing. Plant evergreen trees and shrubs that will provide **COVER** all year. Deciduous shrubs are good for nesting in the summer. Mulch piles, rocks, and logs offer cover for small mammals, reptiles, amphibians, and many insects. Finally, provide **PLACES TO**

RAISE YOUNG by putting out nesting boxes for birds and a pool where tadpoles can turn into frogs or toads, and newts and dragonflies can lay eggs. Many flowers, herbs, and trees can provide both food and shelter for butterflies and moths.

Backyard Wildlife Habitat gardens are not limited to homes. Schools, churches, and businesses are ideal places to make a wildlife habitat. By certifying more than 21,000 backyards and other sites, the National Wildlife Federation has helped to restore at least 50,000 acres of land to wildlife habitat. This helped to offset some of the thousands of acres that are disturbed or destroyed each year for our use.

If you don't have room to do the whole habitat, then try a Carolina Fence™. This zig-zag fence includes cultural and natural elements, such as our state flower, the yellow jessamine vine. A Carolina wren house is attached to one of the posts. Native blue granite can provide a sunning place for the state butterfly, the tiger swallowtail. Along the fence, grow small shrubs, perennials, and annuals that provide food. The South Carolina Wildlife Federation offers plans. Federation offices in other states may have similar programs.

Businesses may participate in the WAIT program (Wildlife And Industry Together), which encourages corporate landholders to consider habitats in their land management decisions. Employees love being able to watch the parade of nature outside their work place windows, and management can significantly reduce costs for water and mowing. Many businesses have also been paired with schools to help them develop such a garden.

To receive your packet of information (including plans and plant lists) and instructions on applying for certification, get in touch with The National Wildlife Federation at 11100 Wildlife Center Drive, Reston, VA 20190.

Two helpful books on the subject are *The Natural Habitat Garden* and *The Natural Garden*, both by Ken Druse. Go ahead, live a little! Take a walk on the wild side.

October

Hope Springs Eternal

My spring bulbs have come. Soon I will be on my hands and knees tucking daffodil and crocus bulbs into their beds for winter — a task that defies all attempts to achieve human comfort. My order of tulip and hyacinth bulbs arrived with them and will chill in our spare fridge for six to ten weeks.

Despite some past failures, each year I plant more bulbs and eagerly await the results with hopeful expectations. It's a bit like Samuel Johnson's observation about a gentleman who had been very unhappy in marriage, and who had remarried immediately after his first wife's death. Johnson called it "the triumph of hope over experience."

Looking back through my gardening journals, I find the sad tales of bulbs that didn't make it, but I also find just enough happy outcomes to sustain me. Some of the daffodils bloomed only the first year and disappeared, perhaps because the variety was not suited to our climate. Daffodils, because they are poisonous, are safe from attack from squirrels. But our furry little friends gobble up crocus bulbs like popcorn. This year I've anchored a section of small-gauge chicken wire over each planting in hopes of affecting a change in their diets. If you have critters that attack your bulbs from underneath, you have a bigger challenge. I have read that putting a layer of small gravel under the bulbs at planting time might help to foil moles and voles. Some people even plant vulnerable bulbs in an underground cage.

If my chicken wire defense is a success, next spring I'll have 100 *Crocus tommasinianus* 'Whitewell Purple', which the catalog claims to be "squirrel resistant." When you plant crocuses, plant them in hundreds to make the best show. The best crocus for naturalizing in the South is *C. tommasinianus* and its hybrids.

Daffodils. My search for daffodils (*Narcissus* species) that will naturalize (spread, come back) for us has led me to new discoveries. At the top of my list to order again is *Narcissus jonquilla floreplana*, an old bulb often called Queen Anne's jonquil. It looks like a small yellow rose, and the fragrance is sweet and wonderful. At ten to twelve inches tall, it is not a big daffodil; but it doesn't have to be. Unusually beautiful, it looked lovely blooming under my oak tree with blue *Muscari armeniacum*, the grape hyacinth.

I also discovered *N.* x *odorus* 'Campernelli'. The campernelle is another heirloom found in many old Southern gardens. Also fragrant (hence, the odorus in the name), it has two to three all yellow jonquilla blossoms with twisted petals and a flared, scalloped cup per stem.

In my little trough garden I grew the miniature daffodil 'Canaliculatus', one of the wild species. Its four to seven sweetly fragrant flowers per stem have yellow cups (coronas) and white petals. In the summer, these bulbs love to bake in the hot sun. They bloom early to midseason and can be forced in pots like paper whites.

Every year I try to increase my numbers of 'Hawera' and 'Quail', two fairly small daffodils that have done very well for me. 'Hawera' has many diminuitive, pale yellow "nodding bells" with several swept back petals per stem. A late bloomer, it grows equally well in the garden, in a pot, or even in a scree.

'Quail', a real winner, blooms a long time, beginning in midseason. Twelve to fourteen inches tall, with two to four flowers per stem, it belongs to the jonquilla group. I grow it with 'Hawera' under a dogwood tree surrounded by holly fern, hydrangeas, and azaleas. Because of a long bloom season, it is still in bloom when 'Hawera' comes out, and the two together make a fine show.

Most of my daffodils are miniatures. While their foliage is curing, it's not the mess you see with the large daffs. Remember not to disturb the foliage on your bulbs before it has turned pale yellow and flopped over. Otherwise you won't get any flowers next year. Let them dry naturally, no cutesy plaited and rolled down bundles.

I do grow a few larger bulbs. One that I inherited in my garden is an old variety called 'Seventeen Sisters' because it has so many sweet, white, fragrant flowers per stem. The plant is sixteen to eighteen inches tall and blooms early to midseason. One catalog lists it as 'Avalanche'.

A daffodil I recently acquired came from a dear friend who was dividing bulbs from an old country house. Commonly called 'Butter and Eggs', it brought back childhood memories of messy balls of green and yellow that never completely opened. But when I saw her specimens, with their many yellow petals completely unfurled, I realized what a gem a flower from a good bulb is. In one catalog it is listed as 'Golden Phoenix'. It may also be called 'Double Incomparabilis'. Rare and hard to find in the trade, it's worth the search.

The large trumpet daffodils don't perform well for our climate. Better choices are the large-cupped narcissuses, including 'Carbineer', 'Ceylon', 'Carlton', 'Mount Hood', 'Professor Einstein', 'Fortune', 'Gigantic Star', 'Barrett Browning', and the old favorite, 'Ice Follies'.

The popular jonquilla cultivars are among the best for us. Try 'Trevithian', 'Pipit', and 'Dickcissel'. Also good are the tazettas, which include 'Paper White'. You can plant these outside for December bloom. 'Grand Primo', reputed to be one of the best daffodils for clay soil, is also in this group.

The cyclamineus daffodils have produced many good hybrids, such as 'February Gold', 'Peeping Tom', 'Jack Snipe', 'Tête à Tête', and 'Jetfire', which I have planted with blue pansies to complement its orange perianth (cup) and yellow petals. The triandrus cultivars are the latest to bloom well for us. *Narcissus triandrus* (Angel's tears) is a wild species that has been a passalong plant for generations.

Tulips. I have had my successes and failures with tulips. After many years of experimenting, I finally found a tulip that blooms late enough to coincide with my Spanish bluebells. It's *Tulipa* 'Marjolein', an orange member of the lily-flowered group. My favorite tulip for window boxes and containers is 'Yellow Present' because it is not too tall. I always fill my whiskey barrel planter with 'Elizabeth Arden', which looks just like a frosted pinkish-red lipstick. Any leftovers shine in beds and containers.

This spring, I planted 'Apricot Parrot', a novelty tulip with fringed edges in a rose, apricot, yellow combination flecked and striped with green. And it's fragrant, too. I grew it in a pot with 'Easter Basket' sweet alyssum.

Double your pleasure with 'New Design' tulip. It boasts beautiful soft-pink flowers and green-and-white variegated foliage that looks good for a couple of weeks after the bloom is over. In my almost-white garden, I grow 'White Triumphator', a tall, lily-flowered group tulip and a late bloomer. My friend Joan Assey's display of these stately tulips in the front yard of her home is simply elegant.

New bulbs that I'm trying this year include an old tulip variety, 'Clara Butt', with salmon-pink blooms. 'Fancy Frills', known as "the best of all fringed tulips," is a two-toned ivory and rosy pink with a whitish crystalline fringe. 'Candy Club' is a yummy-looking bouquet tulip with several pink and white blooms per stem.

Anemones. *Anemone coronaria* bulbs look like dried up raisins. After soaking overnight, they at least look alive, even if you can't tell which end is up. Just plant them on their sides or upside down. (You won't know which is which.) The beautiful lush foliage starts to come up in late February or early March, followed by wave after wave of poppy-like flowers in blue, pink, or white. They are glorious in your borders and make great cut flowers. I tried three colors this year: blue 'Lord Lieutenant', white 'Mount Everest', and rose pink 'Rosea'.

Other Spring Bulbs. Other bulbs that have worked well for me are Spanish bluebell (*Hyacinthoides hispanica*), which blooms later than the daffodils, about the same time as the Reeves spirea (*Spiraea cantoniensis*). The blue grape hyacinth (*Muscari armeniacum*) is easy and reliable. *Muscari latifolium* has larger flower clusters in two shades of blue, but mine didn't come back. I would plant them again just as an annual.

Hyacinths look good for us the first year, and you may get a fair bloom the second year; but for the most part, they are like tulips and should be treated the same as annuals. Some Southerners grow what they call "Snowdrops," but in all probability they are growing summer snowflakes (*Leucojum aestivum*).

One of the most interesting parts of bulb catalogs is the section called "other bulbs." These include alliums, puschkinias, chionodoxas, the common snowdrop (*Galanthus nivalis*), erythroniums, triteleias, brodiaeas, scillas, and ixias, among many others. These are fun to try in small numbers to see how they perform.

Planting Spring Bulbs. The culture of daffodils and other spring bulbs is simple, if you bear in mind that good drainage is essential. Bulbs will rot in waterlogged soil. If your soil is clay, either mix in fifty percent (by volume) compost, aged bark, or similar soil conditioners. You can also try planting them on a slope or in raised flower beds.

An ideal spot for planting bulbs is in existing flower borders, among the perennials. Digging holes for single bulbs in a new area is too much work, even with a bulb-planting tool. I have several bent ones in the garage to prove it. A good steel bulb planter is costly. Better to spend the money on more bulbs and plant them where the soil has already been worked.

To prepare a new bulb bed, cultivate the soil at least ten inches deep. Incorporate a slow-release bulb fertilizer like Bulb Booster® at planting time and then top-dress every year in the fall or in the spring when new growth starts. An annual addition of wood ashes or greensand adds potash. Epsom salts at the rate of one-half cup per ten square feet is supposed to increase the intensity of the flower colors, but I haven't tried this.

As a general rule, plant bulbs at a depth equal to three times the height of the bulb. Water thoroughly and cover the bed with two to three inches of mulch. Keep them watered, but not soggy. Bulbs need good drainage. Plant them with the growing tip up. It's helpful to soak tulip bulbs that have been in the refrigerator.

After bulbs bloom in the spring, their foliage must make food for next year's blooms, so it is critical that you allow the foliage to dry naturally. Do not plait it or tie it down with rubber bands because it needs as much air and light as it can get. A better solution for camouflaging messy bulb foliage is to plant something else to come along after it, such as hosta. At the New York Botanical Garden, there is a long curving walk bordered by daffodils and daylilies, an ideal combination because both are perennial. They bloom at different times; and the daylily foliage hides the curing daffodil foliage. Finally, allow bulb foliage to die completely before cutting it down. The foliage makes next year's bloom. If old clumps need dividing, the time to do it is just as soon as the foliage has cured.

The world of bulbs is large and diverse, but I'm wondering how many more experiments with different varieties my back and knees can take. As I kneel on my foam pad to plant bulbs, I try to think of Rudyard Kipling's words: "Oh, Adam was a gardener, and God who made him sees that half a proper gardener's work is done upon his knees."

Writings about bulbs I've found helpful include *Daffodils for American Gardens*, *Garden Bulbs for the South*, *A Southern Garden*, *The Little Bulbs*, "Gardener's World of Bulbs," and *Bulbs: How to Select, Grow and Enjoy*.

Berries Brighten the Garden

Is your garden too drab in the winter? I just did a walk around mine and decided that I need more plants with berries for winter color. The occasion of the walk was to find something to decorate my Christmas wreath, although it's nice to have berries to decorate the garden and offer food for the birds all winter.

To me, the ultimate plant for berries is a holly. Jim Porter, a Master Gardener and holly expert, wishes that people would plant more of the deciduous hollies. When their leaves are gone, their berries become even more prominent. This sentiment was echoed by landscape architect Elizabeth Rice, who recommends two cultivars of the deciduous holly, *Ilex decidua* 'Warren Red' and 'Council Fire'. She also reminds us that you must have a male and a female holly in order to have berries. As long as there is a male holly blooming in the vicinity the same time of year as your hollies, you should have berries (assuming you have a female plant). It's best to buy them during the time of the year they are fruiting so you can be sure.

Jenks Farmer, former curator of plants at Riverbanks Botanical Garden, likes the familiar American holly (*Ilex opaca*). And if you like yellow berries, *Ilex vomitoria* 'Saratoga' is a possibility. Both are evergreen. A deciduous holly Jenks likes is *Ilex* 'Sparkleberry'. Its shiny red fruits stand out against bare branches and last all winter on a shrub or small tree that will eventually be twelve feet tall.

Much maligned, old-fashioned nandina gets accolades from a Winnsboro Master Gardener, Martha Wilkes. She says "It just brings back a lot of memories for me because my mother used to decorate with it during the holidays." Nandina is also one of Porter's favorite plants, but it's probably gotten a bad rap because it is often pruned incorrectly. The oldest stems should be cut out at ground level and the others pruned at varying heights to maintain the desired layered look.

Rose hips, though technically not berries, remain colorful in winter. Farmer's absolute favorite rose for decorative hips is the old grandiflora 'Queen Elizabeth'. He also recommends *Rosa rugosa*, but many roses will produce colorful fruit if you don't cut off the last crop of flowers in fall.

The list of viburnums with colorful fruit could go on and on, but an especially nice one for our region is the tea viburnum (*Viburnum setigerum*), which has clusters of bright red berries that hold from fall to winter and are also enjoyed by the birds. I have a hedge of *Viburnum tinus* that blooms in late winter to early spring. The blossoms are followed by metallic-blue fruits.

One of my favorite things to use at Christmas is good old red cedar (*Juniperus virginiana*), especially those branches that are loaded with dusky sky-blue berries that look so good in wreaths and arrangements. This tree evokes many fond memories of my childhood on a dairy farm in Chester County, where we looked every December for just the right cedar to cut down as our Christmas tree. Other blue-fruited plants include the frosted-blue clusters of *Mahonia aquifolium*, which Martha Wilkes loves to use in arrangements.

Many other berried plants come to mind, such as the Chinese photinia (not the disease-plagued red tip), with large clusters of dark-red berries. Jenks Farmer says the beautyberry (*Callicarpa sikokiana*) is the best-berried plant at Riverbanks. The other beautyberries have nice fruit, too. He also reminded me of vines that have berries, such as *Parthenocissus henryana*, a form of Virginia creeper. There's also the pyracantha with its orange or red berries, as well as the Southern magnolia with great seedpods that can be sprayed gold to look so elegant with greenery in arrangements. The red berries of our native dogwood are often used as decorations, too. The ubiquitous Burford holly in its regular form (*Ilex cornuta* 'Burfordii'), and the dwarf form *I. cornuta* 'Nana' are overused; yet make excellent hedges and provide lots of berries with winter color for you and the birds.

Compost — Let It Happen

Ah, the sounds of fall are in the air! As the leaves silently float downward, the din of leaf blowers rises ever higher. While not exactly music to my ears, it is, I suppose, a modern marker of the changing seasons. Everybody wants those leaves off their lawns and driveways and in a big pile on the street. But wait! You are throwing away something worth saving. All those leaves can become a major ingredient for a product called Black Gold. It's compost, and it's free. You can make it yourself, and your garden will love you for it. Whether your soil is clay or sand, compost is the ultimate conditioner. It helps clay soil drain better and sandy soil retain moisture.

All good gardeners are interested in soil building. Fran Bull says "The fall is so gorgeous I don't mind grubbing around in the dirt. I try to do things that will make spring easy. I've already spread several inches of compost over the soil in my raised vegetable beds and topped it off with a layer of pine straw. In spring I just push back the straw and it's ready to go."

When you know all the things that can be composted, you will realize that they are all things we throw away. How clever that we can take grass clippings, leaves, household vegetable waste, disease-free garden clippings, weeds that have not gone to seed, and twigs and limbs (if we have a chipper/shredder) and turn them all into an essential gardening product. Just about the only things organic you should keep out of your compost are animal scraps and bones and grease. A properly maintained compost pile will have a nice, clean, earthy smell.

The "Julia Child" Recipe. So how can you make this marvelous stuff for your garden? There are two schools of thought on how to make compost. The gourmet recipe calls for the materials to be arranged in measured layers in a homemade bin or in a fancy, expensive plastic compost tumbler.

Start with a brown layer (twigs, cornstalks, leaves) of coarse materials. These are rich in carbon. Next, add a layer of green material (grass or garden clippings) for nitrogen. The carbon to nitrogen ratio should be about 25:1. Finish the layers with a thin layer of garden soil that contains beneficial bacteria and microorganisms that speed the decomposition. As you build each successive layer, water it just until it is wet through. Don't make it soggy, because air is a necessary ingredient, too. Leave an indentation in the top to catch and hold rainwater.

A compost pile built this way will soon begin heating up. Internal temperatures should reach 140 to 160 degrees in three to four days. To "cook" all the material, turn the pile about once a week, mixing the hot material in the center with the cooler material from the sides. You may need to add more water, especially in the summer when it evaporates. Keep it damp, not wet. This method will make compost fairly quickly, in three or four weeks. It will be a bit faster in a sunny location, but a shady location keeps it from drying out too fast in summer, so put yours where it's most convenient.

The best-looking composting setup I've seen is that of Master Gardener Cal Shadwell. He constructed three bins from wood, side-by-side, each about four feet square. He adds fresh waste material to the first bin, where it begins the process of decomposition. When it's half-finished, he transfers the materials to the second bin to finish breaking down. Finally, he transfers it from the second bin to the third bin, where he stores it until he's ready to use it in the garden.

The "One-Minute Chef" Recipe. The second way to make compost is self-evident in the title of Stu Campbell's book on composting: *Let It Rot*. If you don't have time to pay attention to a compost pile, this may be the method for you. This is composting at its most basic. A pile of leaves, just left in a corner or put in big plastic bags will make a pretty good soil amendment in a year. Almost anything will eventually break down if you just leave it long enough. We don't compost our magnolia or Darlington oak leaves because they take too long to decompose in our small system. Instead, we pile them on the street and let the city do it for us in their gigantic mulch pile.

A simple enclosure, such as one made of hog wire or concrete blocks, open on one side, can make a great compost bin. Ours is just a four-foot-high wire enclosure open on one side. I keep a plastic bucket in the cabinet under my sink for kitchen waste and bury the contents in the compost pile every day or so. One winter, I used my food processor to finely chop all my grapefruit and orange rinds, figuring that the smaller the pieces the faster they would break down. I soon realized, though, that the first thing that was going to break down was my expensive food processor. Now things just have to do it at their own pace.

Occasionally, I sprinkle over the bin a handful of dolomitic limestone and a handful of 10-10-10 fertilizer, but this is not necessary. Wood ashes are also good because they add potash. I empty my compost pile twice a year — once before I rake up fall leaves and again in the spring. You can use compost to side-dress vegetable garden plantings or to top-dress your shrubs, flowers, or lawn.

If you just can't find a spot to make your own, but would still like some compost, you can get it very inexpensively from many municipalities.

Giving Back to Your Yard. So please don't rake those leaves into the storm sewers where they can clog it and cause an overflow. Instead, put your leaves to work for your garden. Just remember that a good mixture of green and brown materials will decompose the fastest. When you compost, you give back to the soil the various nutrients that have been taken from it. And be sure to wear your facemasks and earplugs when you crank up those leaf blowers.

Hedges Hold the Garden Together

Where have all the red tips gone? These ubiquitous Southern hedging plants, *Photinia x fraseri*, have been under siege in recent years from a fungal leaf spot disease that defies all but the most persistent efforts at control. This is a good time to make a case for plant diversity in our neighborhoods. Diseases spread rapidly among susceptible plants when they are overused. By using a wide variety of plants, we can lessen the impact of such diseases and create a more interesting city landscape.

So what does the home gardener looking for suitable hedging material choose? Several important factors will affect your choices. If the purpose of the proposed hedge is to serve as a privacy screen or windbreak along the outside of your property, it must grow fairly tall and thick. Where zoning restrictions limit the height of a wall, a hedge tall enough to hide views from your neighbor's second-story windows can give you privacy.

If you want to separate and define different areas within your garden, choose a medium-height hedge as background for a flower bed or a low hedge as a border for an herb garden.

Next, do your homework. What kind of soil do you have? Is there sun, shade, or a combination? Will you irrigate? Do you want a clipped, formal hedge or a loose informal one? Evergreen or deciduous? Visits to local nurseries with note pad in hand can help you choose the right plant for the right place. Ask the experts for the ultimate size of the hedge plants as well as their cultural needs. Know what is hardy in your climate.

Consider the color of the foliage as well as the leaf size. Small-leafed plants like boxwood are easier to clip into a firm shape than large-leafed ones. Where space is limited, a clipped hedge may be the answer, but on a large property there is more room for a wide, loose screen that requires lower maintenance.

One of the most beautiful plants for a hedge is the Japanese cleyera (*Ternstroemoia gymnanthera*). It grows slowly to about eight feet but can be kept at four to six feet in height. The new foliage has a reddish cast that returns in the fall and winter. It prefers part shade to shade and is amenable to pruning.

Agricultural Extension Service agent Sam Cheatham offers several more choices for hedges in the Midlands. Three
hollies, *Ilex x attenuata* 'Fosteri', *Ilex* 'Nellie R. Stevens', and
Ilex cornuta 'Burfordii', work well as larger hedges. All are
evergreen and bear fruit heavily. The dwarf form of the
Burford holly makes a good medium-height hedge and can
be clipped into a formal shape. It looks wonderful as a background for a flower border.

Other recommended tall hedges include *Camellia
sasanqua*, which has beautiful fall blooms; wax myrtle; tea
olives; and Leyland cypress, all of which can be pruned or
left natural. Of course, there is always the old standby Japanese privet (*Ligustrum japonicum*), which takes sun or shade,
heavy pruning, and any kind of soil except very wet.

The Japanese hollies are very good medium hedge plants.
Ilex crenata 'Convexa' and *I. crenata* 'Compacta' are durable
and readily available. The lower, mounding form of *Ilex
crenata* 'Helleri' makes a fine low hedge that looks best left
in its natural form, but can also be clipped into a tight low
border for a bed.

Jim Martin, former director of Botanical Operations at
Riverbanks Zoo, likes hollies because they are tough and
drought tolerant. "They also make good barrier hedges," says
Jim. Other plants that will form an impenetrable barrier include wintergreen barberry (*Berberis julianae*), which is too
vicious to prune; the thorny eleagnus (*Elaeagnus pungens*),
which makes a huge mounding barrier for the edge of a large
property; or even a trifoliate orange (*Poncirus trifoliata*), with
bare green stems and thorns in winter.

Jim advises care and patience in establishing a good
hedge and says, "It should be viewed as a long-term investment. The speed of growth is inversely proportional to life
expectancy. You should realize that if something can take
over the world in seven years, it's not going to live for fifty
years!"

Many other plants will do well as hedges in different situations. The *Viburnum tinus* is becoming more popular, both in the twelve- to fifteen-foot form 'Robustum', and in the four- to six-foot form 'Compactum'. Both offer evergreen foliage and flat clusters of pink-opening-to-white flowers in late winter, followed by metallic-blue berries.

Old-fashioned *Nandina domestica* makes a lovely soft hedge if properly pruned. Do not shear it across the top, but remove the oldest canes to the ground and prune the others at varying heights to maintain a full, layered look. This is one of the toughest plants available and offers nice spring flowers and beautiful fall red berries. *Abelia* x *grandiflora* is another classic shrub for a hedge. It covers itself with tiny, white, funnel-shaped blooms all summer and fall. The cultivar 'Edward Goucher' has deep-pink flowers. The abelias look best grown in a natural shape with occasional thinning of the oldest shoots and tipping of others.

Even deciduous shrubs, such as forsythia or flowering quince, when properly pruned, will make beautiful blooming hedges in loose mounding shapes.

One of the most attractive and unusual hedges in Columbia is a pineapple guava (*Feijoa sellowiana*) that belongs to Susan and Rick Umbach. It has gray-green foliage with silvery undersides and exotic red and white flowers in spring. Susan prunes it twice a year to maintain its height at about six feet, and reports it seems perfectly hardy after fifteen years.

There are so many more options for hedges. Boxwood is a classic choice, but plant it away from passing dog traffic. Pittosporum makes a gorgeous hedge but cannot be relied upon to be completely cold hardy. So do spend some time investigating before you invest your time and money.

Fall and winter are good times to plant new hedges. Prepare the soil carefully and use a string between two stakes to assure a straight line. Place plants slightly closer together than their mature spread. For a formal clipped hedge, space them about half the distance of their mature spread. To avoid a leggy look after a few years, always prune a formal hedge with the bottom wider than the top so that light can reach all the way to the ground.

The most important thing to remember about a hedge is that it is a living, breathing organism. As such, it requires proper fertilization, watering, and pruning. But the rewards of a soft, green enclosure for your garden are well worth the effort.

In the middle of winter they smile at us with their bright faces, seemingly impervious to the dropping temperatures. From the French "penser," meaning "to think" comes the name for pansy, a tough little hardy annual that brings us garden color from fall through spring. The pansy has a long history. In literature and lore, the pansy has been associated with thoughts, especially thoughts of love. This explains one of the pansy's many common names, Hearts-ease.

In the Shakespearian play, *Hamlet,* the distraught maiden, Ophelia, carries "rosemary, that's for remembrance; . . . and there is pansies, that's for thoughts." Shakespeare turned again to the pansy for symbolism in *A Midsummer Night's Dream.* "The juice of it, on sleeping eyelids laid, will make a man or woman madly dote upon the next live creature that it sees." You can just imagine the fun Shakespeare had with this love potion, which may refer to an ancient Celtic recipe using the pansy's dried leaves.

One Hardy Little Plant. While the pansy may have lost some of its magic in matters of the heart, it continues to please gardeners everywhere. Even after a snowfall, this determined little flower can be seen raising its face again above the melting snow. The plants can survive temperatures as low as zero degrees Fahrenheit, and the flowers are unharmed at fifteen degrees. To say they prefer cool weather is an understatement. Planted in fall, as the heat begins to abate, they will grow and bloom through the winter and give a lovely spring show before the heat returns.

Don't worry if you miss getting your pansies planted before Thanksgiving. They can still be planted through January and into the first of February.

Pansies belong to the genus *Viola*, but the new, smaller pansies are actually called violas and have become very popular. They flower profusely and are the same size as another viola, the Johnny-jump-up, an old favorite. All make good landscape plants.

Series of Pansies. One of the oldest pansy series is Majestic Giant. Their large flowers and long stems make a grand showing, but they are easily beaten down by the rain. Other series with large flowers include Accord and Medallion. In the medium category are Crown, Imperial series (great pastels), Delta, Roc (no faces), Maxim (faces), and Universal (many choices of colors with or without faces). The most popular of the viola series is Sorbet.

Other series of pansies offer smaller blooms, but they are more floriferous and resist weather better. Maxim and Accord series pansies and Sorbet violas have been bred for heat tolerance, meaning you can enjoy them later in the spring. In a catalog, I saw the dramatic 'Springtime Black' and exotic deep orange 'Padparadja' pansies. These should be grown from seed started in early winter or in late summer.

The panola is a cross between the pansy and the viola. One of the best is 'Yesterday, Today, and Tomorrow', so named because flowers turn from white to lavender to purple as they age and make a very pretty combination.

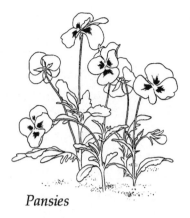

Pansies

Whether you prefer pansies with faces or plain, there are enough variations and colors available to satisfy any planting plan. They are useful as borders and in containers. As my husband observed, "What's great about pansies is that you don't need a big yard — a window box will do."

In the landscape, pansies also make perfect companions for spring bulbs. You can plan your color schemes so the colors of the pansies will complement your daffodils and tulips. Don't worry about disturbing your pansies if you haven't planted all your bulbs yet. You can dig right under them and pop in a bulb. For a bigger show, plant a lot of one color of pansies together. Yellow seems to be the most popular color choice, followed by the mix, then by true blue. If you make your own mix, be sure to use pansies from the same series.

Caring for Pansies. Pansies have very specific needs, but they are not hard to satisfy. You should plant them in well-amended soil (compost added) in full sun for best bloom, or also part shade. You should fertilize them frequently. Water them, but avoid making the soil soggy, and deadhead them (pick off old blooms).

There are many types of fertilizer for pansies. Garden centers sell a granular pansy food to use once a month. Some customers still ask for blood meal, which is used at the rate of one pound per twenty-five pansies. There is also a product called Pansy-Mate that contains what the producer calls "cricket crap," plus lawn clippings, bone meal, and blood meal. Used every thirty days, "it gives you the biggest blooms," says Sherry Bellefontaine. In addition, you can amend the soil with Earth Healer™, a screened form of composted chicken manure. An all-organic concentrated liquid plant food is also available.

Experts recommend feeding your pansies every two to three weeks. Getting out there on a sunny day and picking off the old blooms will help to keep them blooming. Fertilizing the pansies on warm days seems to provide the best results.

Get some pansies or violas and plant them on a mild day. You'll thank yourself this spring. But if you are tempted to use the leaves for an old Celtic love potion, consult your doctor first. He may have a more orthodox prescription.

Adding Fall Color

The evidence mounts that the year is winding down. Daylight begins later and ends sooner. The state fair has come and gone. As I turn the dwindling number of pages on my daily desk calendar, the leaves outside are turning from green to red, orange, yellow, gold, and russet. Once again, nature is presenting a last extravaganza of color before it settles its wintry, gray blanket over us.

As summer flowers fade away, our gardens can put on a Joseph's coat of brightly colored foliage. If you need more plants to enjoy during these crisp autumn days, you can add trees and shrubs with outstanding fall color right now. Fall is a perfect time to plant container and balled-and-burlapped specimens.

The ground is still warm enough to encourage new roots to grow, even though the top of the plant is going dormant.

All winter, the new roots can become established enough to withstand next summer's inevitable trials.

Trees Offering Fall Color. I have been observing the trees that offer the bonus of fall color. Most of us are familiar with some of the best: dogwood, crape myrtle, Japanese maple, eastern redbud, red maple and sugar maple, and red oak and scarlet oak.

But how many Chinese pistachio (*Pistacia chinensis*) trees have you seen? "For the southern states this is the closest thing to rivaling Sugar Maple for fall color," writes Mike Dirr, a highly respected authority on woody plants. Besides tolerating a wide range of soils and conditions, it has no serious disease or pest problems. It is also drought resistant. The best feature of this tree is its brilliant fall foliage of orange and orange-red. Plant it in full sun, and prune it when it is young to develop a nice oval head.

In my front yard, the star magnolia (*Magnolia stellata*) has bright gold leaves. They look pretty against its light green ones as it slowly changes color and disrobes, leaving behind in its fuzzy little buds a promise of spring.

Another splendid tree for fall color is the serviceberry (*Amelanchier arborea*). A tree about the size of a redbud, it has white flowers in spring, interesting bark, and some of the best fall color of any small tree. It also produces small blueberry-like fruits that are tasty enough to make a pie. Naturally, the birds love this tree, too.

The black gum or tupelo (*Nyssa sylvatica*) is often overlooked as an ornamental. However, according to Dirr, it is "one of the best and most consistent native trees for fall color." At thirty feet tall and twenty feet wide, it makes an excellent shade tree for the home garden. Fall colors range from yellow through orange to red and purple.

A small tree that would make a fine garden specimen is the Persian ironwood (*Parrotia persica*). It can be grown in sun or light shade, and is pest resistant. In addition to attractive foliage and bark, it carries its bright yellow to orange to scarlet leaves well into December.

Despite what you may have heard, sugar maple will grow and have good fall color in our zone (7b, 8a). A cultivated variety called 'Legacy' can withstand more stress than the species, and it has beautiful orange-red fall foliage.

Finally, two last trees must be mentioned, mainly because we think of them primarily as spring trees. They are both cherries, the Yoshino and the 'Okame'. Each is glorious in the spring, but they shine again in the fall with attractive leaf color.

Colorful Shrubs for the Fall. We usually don't think of deciduous shrubs as having a good fall display, but there are many possibilities. They stand out in our mixed borders and against the green of our evergreens. A shrub that earns its name, burning bush (*Euonymus alatus*), is aflame with leaves of fiery red that make a sight to behold, especially when used as a hedge. It can also stand alone in the landscape. Preferring full sun, burning bush will still work in shade. It needs moist but well-drained soil, and its shallow roots need protection with a mulch in summer.

Virginia sweetspire (*Itea virginica*) is a large native shrub with panicles of fragrant white flowers in spring. In fall, the foliage goes through an ever changing range of rich hues. In my garden, this shrub remains colorful until the end of December, even retaining a scattering of leaves until spring. A popular cultivar, 'Henry's Garnet', has even better flowers and fall color. As this shrub tends to sucker, it works well for massing. Size of plants ranges from three feet to five feet tall, with a wider spread. It is supposed to require moist soil, but I grow it under a pecan tree in my sandy loam.

In the fall, my fatsias appear in their prettiest dress, with candelabra-like compound umbrels of creamy white flowers. Scattered throughout the dark, shiny, evergreen leaves of Alexandrian laurel (*Danae racemosa*) are striking, large, orange-red berries.

The mophead hydrangeas still have a pinkish-greenish tint. I'm tempted to pick them to take indoors, but I always try to wait until the last minute because I enjoy seeing them outside. The stems are never very long because I cut them back to the first bud, so I won't harm next spring's bloom. Behind these, the oakleaf hydrangea is beginning to turn shades of red, purple, and yellow. The flower heads are still intact and attractive in their tan fall dress.

How about a fruit plant for your landscape? Not only will rabbiteye blueberries (*Vaccinium ashei*) provide you with delicious fruit in summer, they have appealing fall color. Summer foliage on some cultivars is a very pretty blue-green. For best fruit production, you should plant at least two, and preferably three, different varieties. Your local Agricultural Extension Service office has brochures available with suggestions for the best ones for your area.

Other shrubs that provide fall color include the native azaleas, *Lespedeza thunbergii*, several of the barberries, and laceleaf staghorn sumac (*Rhus typhina* 'Laciniata'). Save the last one for an informal or wild area of the garden. But if you've ever seen its glowing red leaves and clusters of burgundy fruit along our highways, you can imagine the possibilities.

Colorful Perennials for the Fall. Perennials have fall color, too. Plumbago (*Ceratostigma plumbaginoides*) and its shrubby cousin, Chinese plumbago (*C. willmottianum*), look their best at this time of the year. Their cerulean blue flowers are set against leaves that alternate in color from green to red.

The amsonias also have lovely color in autumn, particularly *Amsonia hubrectii*. Its willow-like green leaves turn bright yellow, the same color as the dying foliage of my hostas. My white variegated ligularia (*Ligularia tussilaginea* 'Argenteum') recently produced its first yellow composite flower. It's nice, but the foliage alone is reason enough to grow this perennial, as well as its other forms. One look at the irregular, round, yellow spots on its green foliage explains why the common name of *L. tussilaginea* 'Aureo-maculatum' is leopard plant.

My pineapple sage (*Salvia rutilans*) is in full bloom with scarlet red flowers. When crushed, its leaves smell like pineapple. I've never understood why this plant is sold in some catalogs as "Hummingbird Plant," as it's pretty late in the year for any hummers to still be hanging around. I would grow it just to be able to rub a leaf every time I pass by and get my pineapple fix.

It's still a while until the season's first hard freeze, when all this color will be gone. Some gardeners may choose to begin cleaning up their flower beds soon, but I'll be among the procrastinators. I want to enjoy the color as long as I can. We're blessed with enough mild, winter days when I can tidy up the garden.

November

Fall's Sensory Delights

Fall is rich with sensory delights — a bite into a crisp mountain apple; the taste of fragile, fragrant raspberries that fall into your hand and stain it deep red; the little nip in the air; the bright colors of tree leaves glowing in the fall sunshine; the roadsides decorated with fall asters, goldenrod, and blooming grasses; mountains that turn into a patchwork of reds, yellows, and oranges set off by the bluest of blue skies where hawks, and sometimes eagles, soar over the heights.

By now you've probably guessed that my husband and I were in the mountains this past weekend. On the way home, I couldn't help trying to remember what colors and scents would greet me when I got back to my fall garden. Does it have enough sensory delights?

Is there enough fall color from shrubs like barberry, itea, lespedeza, winged euonymus, the russet red and yellow leaves of oakleaf hydrangea, and Chinese or American forms of the beautyberry? Are they sited to best advantage, perhaps against an evergreen background? I'm sure nurseries are stocked with plenty of these shrubs, and it's fortunate that this happens to be the perfect time of year to plant them.

Trees can be planted now, too, and the list of those with colorful foliage is long. It includes familiar favorites like crape myrtles, dogwoods, and redbuds, as well as Chinese pistachio, black gum, gingko biloba, 'Okame' cherry, sugar maples, Chinese tallow tree (popcorn tree), Japanese maples, red oaks, sweetgum, black gum, and bald cypress. Fall is a great time to plant these, too.

As for fall scents, I'm fortunate to be able to enjoy my neighbor's tea olive this time of year. Roses should respond to the cooler temperatures by filling the air with fragrance one more time before winter. And wouldn't you guess that fall is a perfectly wonderful time to plant roses? It would be lovely to be greeted in the mornings by the perfume of moon-flower vine or angels' trumpets. My sasanquas (*Camellia sasanqua*) are just beginning to bloom, filling my sitting garden with the sweetest scent. If you are planning to plant a sasanqua camellia this fall, buy it while it is in bloom so you can see and smell the flowers.

In the fall flower garden there are many possibilities for color, from both blooms and foliage. The purple and white Mexican sage is at its peak now. In fact, most perennial salvias have been with us all summer and will bloom until frost. If Japanese anemones have made it through the searing heat and drought of this past summer, they will send up their pastel, delicate blooms. The most reliable of these seem to be *Anemone hupehensis* 'September Charm' and *A. x hybrida* 'Honorine Jobert'.

Ceratostigma plumbaginoides and wild blue ageratum (a thug you can't get rid of so you might as well enjoy it) provide a welcome touch of blue among all the reds, oranges, and yellows of the tall sunflowers (helianthus), and the heliopsis and amsonia foliage.

The curious toad lilies (*Tricyrtis hirta*) are now in bloom. They compel you to inspect their oddly beautiful little flowers at closer range. Plant them in your shade garden.

The ornamental grasses are in their glory now as they come into flower. The most beautiful combination I've seen was a planting of the burgundy red flowers of *Salvia vanhouttii* in front of the maroon tassels of 'Gracillimus' miscanthus. The colors seemed to reflect each other and double the effect.

It would be hard to write about fall color without mentioning mums — conventional and mundane, yet still beautiful and irresistible. Tending to choose the new and exotic over the tried and true, I may resolve not to succumb to mums this year. But who can withstand the allure of the kaleidoscopic selection of colorful mums that tempt you everywhere you turn, from the supermarket to roadside stands, as well as at garden centers and nurseries? When it comes to mums, I have to decide how much I'm willing to spend for a plant I treat as an annual, much like tulips. For a few dollars you still get three or four weeks of color, which is not a bad return on your investment.

Even vegetables get into the act. Cabbage, kale, and red mustard may sound like a salad, but these, along with the 'Bright Lights' chard with its red, yellow, orange, or pink stems, can add color to containers and beds all winter.

Flowers and shrubs offer a smorgasbord of fall sensory pleasures, but what can top the gooey feel of pumpkin seeds as you pull them out of the prospective jack-o'-lantern? Doubtlessly, the smells, sounds, and sights that say "fall" better than anything else are found at the state fair. The award-winning displays of produce, the best flowers from gardens all over the state, all overlaid with the fragrances of elephant ears, Polish sausages, and Fiske fries; and above it all, the familiar sounds of the public address announcer saying, "Billy Bob, meet your mother at the Rocket."

Winter Fragrances

I caught a whiff of it in the air while out walking. A fragrance so sweet you have to find its source. Like gardenias, but you know it's too late for them. Looking around, you may see only evergreen shrubs or bare limbs. Look a little closer and you will find tiny, brown-speckled, bell-shaped white flowers hiding in the deep green and silver leaves of *Elaeagnus pungens*, a large, late-fall-blooming shrub. Somewhat unruly in its habit of sending out long branches in every direction, it can make a good screen at the edge of the property and provide great cutting material for arrangements. Then, there's this fall bonus of flowers that will scent the whole garden.

In my garden right now, the sasanqua camellias are blooming. My shrubs are large and old. When they are in full bloom in the fall, they look like gigantic rose bushes smothered in pink or white blooms, which scent the whole garden. All sasanquas are not fragrant, though, so if fragrance is what you want, buy them while they are in bloom. My three pink ones are fragrant, but the white one is not, though I don't think my sampling is large enough to make any kind of judgment.

My neighbor has a huge old tea olive (*Osmanthus fragrans*) just on the other side of the fence. It is my good fortune to be able to enjoy its sweet scent. Its unobtrusive clusters of small white flowers can scent the air for a long distance. This shrub has the added bonus of blooming several times between fall and spring. Catching a whiff of tea olive in bloom when I walk out the back door is always a delightful surprise. It's a lovely day-brightener.

There are enough fall and winter fragrances to keep you following your nose around your garden at a time of year when blooms are scarce. The reason you don't find more plants with winter fragrances in gardens is, ironically, because of the time of year they bloom. Many people don't think of going to the garden center in winter, when these and other plants are in flower, so they don't see and smell them when they are in bloom. Therefore, the nursery owner hesitates to invest in plants that may not sell. For that reason, wonderful winter-blooming plants, such as winter hazels and witch hazels, are hard to find. But if you know to ask for them and search diligently, you can usually find what you want. If you don't have any luck locally, try a specialty catalog.

The witch hazel (*Hamamelis* species and cultivars) is one of winter's best-kept secrets. With careful selection, you could enjoy various ones throughout the winter, as different cultivars come into bloom. Although the flowers are not large, they can pack a powerful scent into their little clusters of crinkly, strappy petals. Various cultivars have been bred for larger flowers with more color, but the species *Hamamelis virginiana* still offers one of the strongest fragrances.

Good varieties of *Hamamelis* x *intermedia* to look for include 'Arnold Promise', with yellow flowers in February and beautiful yellow leaves in fall. 'Diane' is a good red-flowering form, with rich fall coloring of red, yellow, and orange foliage. Another good selection is 'Jelena', with excellent coppery colored flowers that are faintly scented, but the fall color is spectacular. Eminent plantsman Michael Dirr laments the lack of use of these "lovely, maintenance-free plants."

Even less well known is the winter hazel (*Corylopsis* species). Most are shrubs of spreading habit with fragrant yellow flowers on short racemes in late winter and early spring. Two of the best for the garden are the buttercup winter hazel (*C. pauciflora*) and the spike winter hazel (*C. spicata*). These are fairly large spreading shrubs. They will show to best advantage if sited in front of an evergreen background to set off their unusual flowers and fall color.

Mahonia aquifolium will soon be producing its fragrant clusters of small yellow flowers that are followed by frosty blue berries resembling a bunch of grapes. This evergreen shrub has long compound leaves with spiny leaflets that look like holly, thus the common name Oregon grapeholly. It adds a nice texture to a shady shrub border in addition to producing winter flowers and berries. Many other species of mahonia exist. This is just the most common.

A large winter-blooming shrub that I look forward to

each year is the winter honeysuckle (*Lonicera fragrantissima*). It carries its tiny, white, waxy, lemon-scented flowers from January through March in this region. It is almost evergreen, keeping some of its leaves all winter. But the flowers are the reason to grow this, again in the back of the border, where it can spend the summer just being green background. There is a large old specimen in my neighborhood, and I can't walk by without burying my nose in the foliage. People driving by must wonder what on earth I'm doing. I'm sure I look as if I'm getting drunk on perfume.

Another back-of-the-border large shrub is the winter-sweet (*Chimonanthus praecox*), whose name tells you that it blooms early. It is often cut for forcing into even earlier bloom inside. Again, this shrub shines when most needed, in the dead of winter, but fades into the background in summer.

Some fragrant plants should be located close to entrances, where you will enjoy them as you come and go. My favorite for this role is the winter daphne *(Daphne odora)*, a handsome shrub year-round, but a sensation when it blooms in February. It bears beautiful clusters of white or pink flowers with an intoxicating citrusy smell, depending on the cultivar. *Daphne odora* 'Aureomarginata' has leaves outlined in yellow and flower clusters of pink and white. Because it is just as pretty in bud as in bloom, I like this one best. It is an aristocratic shrub that no garden should be without, despite its finicky behavior (it sometimes dies almost overnight for no apparent reason). Just buy another one. Its scent is worth it.

Even bulbs and herbaceous plants provide winter fragrance. Paper white narcissuses don't have to be planted inside in a container of rocks. They will bloom for years in your garden around Christmas time.

Soon after Christmas, the small fragrant daffodils, jonquilla and tazetta types, begin to bloom. Finally, evergreen herbs like rosemary and lavender yield their pungent scents if brushed by your clothing.

When planning a garden, we usually think first in terms related to our visual sense. We consider plants or shrubs on the basis of the color of their blooms and foliage. But it is the fragrances that evoke the strongest response. The sense of smell is the sense that most often stirs memories from the past, often of delightful plants we remember from childhood. Plant now for pleasant memories in the future.

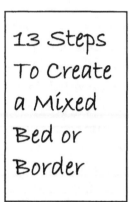

13 Steps To Create a Mixed Bed or Border

Fall is a good time to make new beds and borders. Just because those overgrown azaleas were there when you bought the house, you don't have to keep them for another twenty years. You won't hurt their feelings if you pull them out and throw them away. Or better yet, you could grind them into compost to put on your new bed.

Prepare your site now, and you can spend the winter planning what to put in it. It's a good project for those cold or rainy winter days. Here's how to do it:

1. Choose a site. A sunny spot will give you more plant options, but shade is a possibility, too. Decide which vantage point will be best for viewing your bed or border. You want to be able to see it. Most people use the terms "bed" and "border" interchangeably to mean a place where flowers are planted. A border should border something, like a fence, a wall, a walk, or a hedge. A bed, such as an island bed, may be free floating, with grass paths all around it. But it must be sited carefully so that it doesn't look adrift.

A bed should relate to the rest of the garden in scale. An island bed can make a small garden look larger, especially if you can look through the bed and see that there is more garden to explore. Island beds can make a large garden seem more intimate by breaking up the space. This also means less grass to mow.

2. Pick a theme and/or a season. The theme for your bed or border could be a particular color or combination of colors that appeals to you. Or the theme could center around a favorite plant, such as daylilies. They can be planted with companion plants that bloom at the same time.

If you have a large yard, you might choose a single season for your border. A border that is resting will not be noticed as much in a large yard as in a small one. Most people want interest for more than one season, and this requires a larger border. In a mixed border you can plant shrubs (evergreen and deciduous), even a small tree, as well as perennials, annuals, grasses, bulbs, and vines. Anything goes, and the deeper the border, the more options you have. An eight- to twelve-foot-deep border can accommodate a lot of plants.

3. Decide whether you will have a border with a background or an island bed that is open to view from all sides. The flowers in a border should not clash with the color of the background. In an island bed, you have more freedom with your color scheme. A small island bed can have one high point; a larger one, several. Balance a tree on one end with a group of shrubs or an ornamental grass at the other end. Repeat some plants from the rest of your garden to give a sense of unity.

4. Fit the style of the bed or border to the style of your house. Cottages call for informal planting. A formal house needs a more formal design, such as symmetrical plantings and square or round shapes.

5. Know the plants. Become familiar with your raw materials — the plants. Visit friends' gardens and botanical gardens, and study books and catalogs with pictures, sizes, and cultural information.

6. Lay out your proposed bed. Use a garden hose that has softened in the sun. If you have a two-story house, look at the site from an upstairs window. Think of your curves as part of larger circles, not wimpy, squiggly lines. Try to make your proportions look right with the rest of the garden. Don't be too skimpy.

7. Take soil samples from the site to your local Agricultural Extension Service office. Have your soil analyzed before you get ready to prepare it. The turn-around time is usually about two weeks. You can add any recommended soil amendments when you prepare the soil.

8. Photograph the area you have marked off with the hose and measure it. You can mark your line with horticultural spray paint or powdered lime. Draw the bed to scale on graph paper. This is your base map. Using tissue overlays, begin to sketch in your plants with circles for trees and shrubs and long narrow drifts for perennials. Plan color for several seasons by putting each season on a separate overlay. For your final planting plan, combine all the overlays.

9. Put shrubs or small trees into your plan first. Then add any ornamental grasses or architectural plants, such as yuccas or large mulleins. Strive for interesting combinations of foliage and flower shapes. Don't have all daisy shapes or all spikes. Include evergreen as well as deciduous plants. Plant in odd numbers (three, five, etc.), in irregularly shaped clumps, or in long narrow drifts. Fill in bare spaces, such as under deciduous shrubs, with spring bulbs. Annuals for extra seasonal color can be tucked in anywhere you need them.

10. Figure out the numbers of plants you will need. Refer to information in plant books or read the labels at the nursery to determine the mature sizes. If you can buy all the plants at once (Oh, joy!), bring them home and place them on top of the bed according to your plan. Adjust any you think need it. If you can afford to buy only some of the plants, buy the larger ones, like shrubs or small trees, first. Later you can buy the perennials and wait for them to multiply, filling in your bed or border with annuals in the meantime.

11. Prepare your soil. Always locate water, sewer, gas, and power lines before you do any serious digging. If there is sod on the site, get rid of it. Round-Up® will kill it when it is in active growth. Or cut the grass with a flat sod cutter, just at the point where the roots meet the stolens. Either use the sod in other places or compost it.

Now, using the results from your soil test, add any recommended amendments, plus two to three inches of compost, and till the soil to a depth of eight to ten inches. Let it rest and settle for a few days, or even until early next spring. Install irrigation and put in any type of edging you have chosen. Plant the plants no deeper than they were growing in their containers.

12. Add decorative ornaments if you like. Use your imagination to place a piece of statuary, a bird bath, an urn, or a tuteur with a gazing globe to reflect a dominant color. The possibilities are endless. This gives the garden more structure and more interest in winter.

13. Don't worry if you don't get everything right the first time. You can correct many things with a pencil on your plan. Even after plants are in the ground, they are fairly easy to move, and you can't hurt their feelings by pitching one you really don't like. A shovel is your best design tool. Even if certain things don't work out, you have learned something. Experiment. The process itself is important. This is half the fun of gardening, and that's what it's all about — having fun.

Crabapples
and
Cherries

If you've been wondering how you could add a splash of spring color to that drab part of your yard or garden, consider planting a crabapple or ornamental cherry tree. Do it now, and the gift you give yourself will keep giving, year after year.

Crabapples. Many crabapples offer beautiful flowers and colorful leaves, and the fruit can be made into jelly or jam. Some bear yellow fruit, but most are red. The birds love the fruit, too, so you must be both vigilant and agile if you want to collect enough fruit for a recipe.

Crabapples begin blooming in spring at an early age. They bloom after the flowering cherries and before the dogwoods. You seldom see crabapples in gardens because many are susceptible to problems. However, plant breeders have successfully worked to create disease-free ones. In just one of my plant encyclopedias, I have found numerous such varieties. Here are a couple of good examples.

Malus hupehensis, or tea crabapple, has light-pink buds fading to pinkish white. Its yellow fruit turns red and persists into winter. The tree is vase-shaped and has very good disease resistance.

Malus 'Donald Wyman' offers a single expanded flower bud colored from red to pink to white. A spreading tree, it has shiny dark green foliage and good disease resistance.

Ornamental Cherries. The spring show in my garden wouldn't be the same without my two cherries. The first to take center stage is the autumn-flowering cherry (*Prunus* x *subhirtella* 'Autumnalis'). Don't let the name fool you — it blooms in the winter and spring as well as in the autumn.

Although cherries are often described as short-lived, the subhirtella types are among the most cold hardy and are heat and stress tolerant. There is a lovely weeping form that grows very fast. Some years, my autumn-flowering cherry blooms before Christmas, and other years it waits until after the first of the year. It can bloom several times, usually after a mild period preceded by a very cold spell. This early bloom-ing will not diminish the spring bloom, as with other flow-ering trees.

Another worthy cherry is the 'Okame'. Its fairly narrow growth habit is more upright than that of most cherries. Mine grows along my driveway so I can drive right by it and en-joy its blooms. All through the spring, it is covered in car-mine-rose flowers. In autumn the foliage is attractively col-ored.

A much-loved ornamental cherry is the Manchu, or Nanking, cherry. It can be twelve feet tall and grows up to sixteen feet broad. Its bark is shiny, and its leaves are shiny bright green and very fuzzy underneath. With pink fragrant flowers that fade to white, it also offers shiny red fruit and yellowish fall color.

A gift to America nearly a century ago from the people of Japan, the Yoshino cherry tree graces the Tidal Basin in our nation's capital. In the Midlands, Yoshinos bloom with forsythias in late winter, and are usually the earliest flower-ing trees. They bloom profusely in sun and very respectably in partial or high shade.

The Yoshino cherry grows very fast, up to two feet a year. It can be planted in average soil, if it has good drainage with medium moisture. Growing in height and in spread to twenty to thirty feet, it bears very fragrant, translucent, pale-pink or white flowers.

Thanks to the efforts of Margaret Williams, Orangeburg has undertaken a citywide planting of Yoshino cherry trees. If you want a spectacular show, just take a trip to Orangeburg while the forsythias are in bloom.

Pots and Plans for the Winter

Gardeners plan ahead. A friend recently asked me, "What can I put in all my empty pots for winter interest?" I had a few ideas, but I've learned from other gardeners that the possibilities are almost limitless.

The urn in my back yard is a major focal point, so I always try to fill it with something interesting. This fall, it's curly-leaved green-and-white kale, surrounded by variegated green-and-white 'Glacier' ivy and some white pansies.

Two large, square, concrete planters on either side of my back door contain giant liriope year round. In summer, the liriope provides a backdrop for colorful pots of flowers arranged on the steps below. In winter, it holds down the fort with its evergreen foliage.

Two large pots on my front porch have permanent clumps of variegated aspidistra. After I remove the coleuses, caladiums, and impatiens of summer, I plant tall tulips for spring and overplant these with pansies and Korean rock fern. A green ivy drapes over the sides. Two English boxwoods grow in containers placed inside the borders of my sitting garden. They become part of the winter structure of the garden.

Gardener Jim Porter says he grows almost everything in pots because many plants do better there than in the ground. Daphne is a good example. "It may grow even better in a pot," he says, "and it grows so slowly that it can remain there." After losing three daphnes myself, I am ready to pot my next one, too. Though daphnes are finicky, sometimes dying practically overnight for no apparent reason, nothing in February compares with the beauty and fragrance of a daphne in bloom. Use one close to an entrance where you will enjoy it every time you come and go.

Other suggestions from Jim Porter included the small

'San Gabriel' nandina, which colors nicely in the winter. You could plant a complementary color of pansies around it. "*Rohdea japonica* makes a nice winter hardy pot plant, as would the evergreen holly fern," he adds.

Another friend with great ideas, Hannah Rogers, grows a loropetalum in a large container on her front steps. For several years it has sported lovely burgundy leaves and

Euonymus

bright-pink fall and spring flowers. "You can whack it back any time it gets out of bounds, too," she says. Hannah also grows many winter annuals in pots. She said godetia (also known as clarkia) survived two weeks of being covered by ice and snow and still looked beautiful in spring. In protected areas, alyssum, petunias, and lobelia do well. Fragrant, small white nemesia bloomed all last winter. Hannah also suggests stock, another fragrant winter annual, as well as the foliage of painted daisies, *Artemisia lactiflora*, and snapdragons. Shrubs, such as sasanqua camellia, tea olive, and variegated euonymus also do well in containers.

Many perennial herbs will live happily in pots in winter. Parsley and rosemary look good with flowering winter annuals, and their evergreen foliage is a beautiful foil for spring bulbs. Golden feverfew looks lovely with blue or purple pansies.

Why not use vegetables in your winter containers? 'Red Bor' kale, 'Red Bowl' lettuce, Swiss chard with green or multicolored stems, and 'Osaka' red mustard mix happily with calendulas, wallflowers, or pansies.

Finally, why not plant a Christmas-tree-shaped evergreen

shrub and decorate it with lights for the holidays? Many would work. Just walk around your local garden center and make your choice. When spring comes, you can plant it in your garden. In our climate, there is no reason you can't have something interesting in your containers throughout the year.

December

Santa's Garden Helper

It was my favorite gardening tool, a poacher's spade from Smith & Hawken, and it was gone! With its stirrup handle and long, narrow, curved blade, it was perfect for digging in a perennial border. So when my daughter Eveleigh asked me what I would like for Christmas, I had the perfect answer.

In addition to special-purpose spades, smaller digging tools such as trowels and dibbles in various sizes make great gifts. So would a pair of hand pruners. My Felco pruners and I are almost joined at the hip, but Corona makes a good bypass pruner as well. A ratchet pruner that's easy on the wrists is inexpensive. A holster for hand pruners will save the gardener's pockets and help him or her keep up with the tools better. Any number of other hand tools would be welcome gifts. Look for trowels and small forks and weeders of carbon steel or other heavy metal with sturdy wooden handles that won't bend or break.

Another favorite gardening tool is a narrow cast-metal trowel that is truly unbendable. It's great for planting small bulbs or setting out bedding plants. I also couldn't get along without my small transplant spade, which is great for moving perennials and small shrubs. Gardening enthusiast extraordinaire Phillip Jenkins likes a thirty-inch spade that he can use while on his knees and still get good leverage.

My favorite among an array of neat carriers for tools is a sturdy styrofoam bucket outfitted with a cloth tool caddy around the outside. A friend has one; and I like the way the inside can keep a drink cold, or hold weeds, clippings, or cut flowers. Put the lid on and it becomes a resting place for a tired gardener.

After visiting some garden centers and browsing through a stack of catalogs, I've concluded that a very practical gift would be a large, collapsible bag with handles to hold debris from pruning, weeding, or cleaning out beds. I have one called a Bosbag® that's made of sturdy material and folds up to about the size of an umbrella. You'd be amazed at how much it can carry, and its plastic ribs hold it wide open for that first armful of debris.

A good watering can is worth its weight in gold. Some of the pricier ones, such as the perfectly balanced Hawes watering cans from England, cost almost that much. Just think of it as a once-in-a-lifetime investment. A Hawes watering can might have to be ordered from a catalog.

There are lots of inexpensive watering cans, too. All are useful, from little ones for watering African violets in the house to three-gallon ones for heavy watering in the garden. I just lost one of my large plastic ones to old age. Because I have three outdoor spigots, I like to have a watering can stashed out of sight at each one.

Besides using the right tool for the job, gardeners must also dress for success. A spiffy garden theme T-shirt or sweatshirt gets me in the mood, especially if I'm going to work in our neighborhood park or at the school. When gardening, I usually wear plastic garden clogs with a pull-out cork liner. Afterwards, I hose them down and leave them by the back door. Slip on heavy socks made especially for clogs or use other heavy washable ones.

On my hands, I wear cotton gloves for light weeding and pruning; or heavy, rubber-coated gloves for pruning roses. (And your mom goes through several pairs of gloves a year, Bret.) Janice Beatty, a Master Gardener, raved about gloves that a friend had found in Atlanta. "They are marvelous, good for all kinds of gardening except roses. A rubber material covers palms and fingertips, and a stretchy fabric top keeps hands cool." The gloves, in sizes from small to extra large, are called "Grip."

"Half a proper gardener's work is done upon his knees," so look for pads that strap around the knees with velcro and don't fall off. I don't know about you; but my knees can't take the brick path or concrete drive, or even the lawn anymore. These cushions move right along with you, keeping your hands free and making your work much more pleasant. I also use a kneeling pad. When I'm planting bulbs, I appreciate my kneeling bench with side handgrips. Flip it over and it becomes a stool.

A watering timer, a brass nozzle for the hose, a good doormat that scrubs shoes clean, or a soil thermometer for judging when the soil is warm enough to plant — each comes in handy. Most garden centers have these items.

If you have a friend who tries to have the earliest tomatoes each year, get him a set of "Wall O' Water®." Made of plastic pockets that you fill with water and surround the plant to keep in warmth, it allows tomatoes to go into the ground up to eight weeks early. To give your friend a tool to test the ground for the perfect time to plant outside, how about a soil thermometer?

Plants are always a perfect gift for a gardener. What about a nice houseplant in a basket, or a potted amaryllis, or paper white narcissus bulbs? I've put together gift baskets containing various gardening supplies, such as plant labels, stretchy plant ties, coated wire, hooked masonry nails for vines, and staking devices. Add a bar of gardener's hand soap and a soft nailbrush.

You can really get carried away in the garden ornaments department. I've never seen so many ways to decorate a garden without digging or sweating! Containers and urns come in every size and shape. So do statues and birdbaths. There are printed signs to catch the eye, wind chimes to catch the ear, and even molded and painted flying fish and rabbits to catch the imagination.

For days when the weather's too bad to garden, a book about gardening makes a perfect gift. Look for gardening books with a Southern bias. (This is not England!) *The Southern Gardener's Book of Lists* by Lois Trigg Chaplin is one of the most helpful books I know for choosing plants for any gardening situation.

Tickets to a gardening lecture at Riverbanks Botanical Garden or your local equivalent would make a dandy gift. If your spouse is a gardener, you could really be a hero with tickets to accompany him or her to Callaway Gardens' annual Southern Gardening Symposium in beautiful Pine Mountain, Georgia. It's the highlight of my winter gardening season!

Gift subscriptions to gardening magazines are always appreciated, and they can be ordered by telephone. As you may know, the gardening pages of *Southern Living* are close to my heart. Other favorites include *Carolina Gardener, Fine Gardening,* and *Horticulture.*

Perhaps the best idea for a very serious gardener is a load of manure. That's right! Especially if it is delivered to the backdoor in time for top-dressing those beds before spring. Look for local sources under "Topsoil" in your Yellow Pages.

Finally, there's always the gift certificate to a favorite nursery, garden center, or mail-order catalog store. Have a wonderful holiday season!

Holiday Decorations from the Garden

We residents of the Deep South are so fortunate. We are blessed with a climate that makes it possible to grow a huge number of evergreen shrubs and trees. Even in the winter, we can find plenty of pretty and unusual material in our gardens to decorate our homes for the holidays. I'd like to share with you some of my favorite ideas.

You can easily make your own wreath for the front door from cuttings of different evergreen shrubs. Good candidates include boxwood, cedar, pittosporum, magnolia, pine, and aucuba. I usually use boxwood, cedar with its frosty blue berries, and a few clippings from my Christmas tree (a Fraser fir) for a nice mix of textures and colors. Other possibilities include pine, holly, loquat, laurel, pineapple guava, and eucalyptus. All of these will hold up better in your wreath or arrangement after an overnight soaking in a bucket of water, or in an extra sink, or even in the bathtub. This is called "conditioning" your plant material. Drop a few blocks of oasis (water-holding foam) in with them to use in other decorations.

To make your own wreath, buy a straw wreath form in the desired size, metal U-shaped pins, wooden picks with wire attached, a spool of wire, and ribbon for a bow from a floral supply house. First, make a hanger with the wire and wrap it around the top of the wreath. If you like the look of magnolia leaves surrounding the wreath, put them on now. Attach them with the U-pins, letting them overlap just a bit. Now turn the wreath over and begin attaching your greenery (using pieces about five to six inches long). Form the greens into clusters and attach them to the wreath with the U-pins, covering the stems of one cluster with the foliage of the next. Work in one direction. (I go counterclockwise because I'm right-handed.) You may mix your greens or use all of one kind, covering the whole wreath form.

Now comes the fun part, adding your own touches. You can be very creative by using dried material like hydrangea blooms, any kind of berries, pods, cones, or fruit. If you like, you can spray them gold or silver by using floral spray paint. Attach these with the wooden picks. Now you can add a bow and it's ready to hang. I have been doing this for years and I've never made the same wreath twice. I've used dried okra pods, popcorn plant, cotton bolls, rose hips, nandina and holly berries, silk flowers, dried flowers, and anything else that looked festive.

Wreath of fruit

It's amazing how many things become so elegant when sprayed with gold or silver paint. Try it on magnolia leaves and pods, hydrangea, pine cones, or sweetgum balls. Use your creativity. I become a mad woman when I have a can of spray paint in my hand.

If you don't want to go to the trouble of making your own wreath, buy a ready-made one from the Christmas tree lot, and then add your own personal touches. I like to make my own so I can have mixed greens. I do this just for the front door. For other places, such as the gate or the back door, you can get a ready-made wreath with a bow.

To make your own holiday arrangements, put some wet oasis in a pretty container and stick in your greens. Nothing could be simpler than a big basket of magnolia leaves or pine boughs with a red bow tied onto the handle.

To make a mantel arrangement without a container, put

a sheet of green plastic-coated florist paper, cut to fit, on each end of the mantel. Wrap a block of wet oasis in more florist paper, and put it on top of the first paper. This will protect your mantel from water damage. Now stick in the greens. Use a knife or pick to punch holes in the oasis if your greenery won't go through the paper. Here's even more opportunity to be creative. For height, you can use tall, bare branches sprayed gold, gold magnolia pods, gold teasel, gold or colored Christmas tree balls, poinsettia blooms, candles, fruit, favorite objects, and greenery.

One year I tried an old-fashioned method of preserving camellia blossoms in wax. You must take great care in melting the wax on the stove so that it doesn't catch fire. It must be warm enough to melt the wax but cool enough so that it won't scorch the camellias. The flowers were so beautiful that I used them on my mantel and my dining room table, where they lasted all through the holidays. Plain camellias, of course, have always been perfect for holiday arrangements. The huge red camellia right outside my dining room window conveniently blooms from December to March. So, I just throw open the shutters, and voila, my dining room is decorated. Well, almost. I will cut some camellias to bring inside for the table.

If you have been saying to yourself as you read this article, "But I don't have any of that in my garden," then it may be time to make some changes. Keep summer flower arrangements and Christmas decorations in mind as you plant your garden.

Have fun creating decorations from material found right there in your garden. The only limit is your imagination.

Essential Books for the Southern Gardener

What does a gardener do in the winter? On days when it's too cold and raw to work outside, I read about gardening and rest my back. Recently, I haven't had much time to read. There have simply been too many beautiful days for gardening. But as winter approaches, I look forward to spending some time beside our fireplace with my books, which are like old friends that I try to visit as often as possible. With the holiday season in mind, I hope you might even find a few gift suggestions for yourself or your favorite gardener.

You will be amazed when you visit your local bookstore and see how much the garden book section has expanded in recent years. Many of my favorite books have been around for a long time; others are recent publications. I intended to give you a list of good books in several categories. However, I soon abandoned that idea after counting all the books I can't live without. Reluctantly, I have pared down the list to a more manageable number.

Good reference books and good bedside reading books are essential for any gardener's library. I begin with Lois Trigg Chaplin's indispensable *The Southern Gardener's Book of Lists: The Best Plants for All Your Needs, Wants, and Whims* (Taylor, 1994). More than 200 lists can help you select plants for any situation. I always check here first when I'm racking my brain for what to plant in a particular spot. It's nice to know that many suggestions came from some of the South's best gardeners.

Two plant books, each written by a University of Georgia horticulture professor, describe most of the plants in Chaplin's book and more. Michael Dirr's *Manual of Woody Landscape Plants* (Stipes, 1998, 5th ed.) covers over 9,400 species and cultivars of trees and shrubs, often with opinionated comments that will have you cackling. It's one of the few really big books I know that has no color pictures, yet it makes you feel you know the plant being described. Bonnie Dirr's line drawings throughout are very helpful.

Dirr's colleague, Allan Armitage, wrote 1,141 pages on *Herbaceous Perennial Plants: A Treatise on their Identification, Culture, and Garden Attributes* (Varsity, 1989). The latest edition adds many new cultivars, all with information about soil and climatic conditions for optimum growth. Many of these plants have been tested in the Athens trial gardens of the University of Georgia. Don't be put off by the hefty size. This book is accessible to beginning and advanced gardeners.

Three other publications target the average homeowner but contain much useful information for gardeners of all levels. Each is edited by Steve Bender, senior garden writer for *Southern Living*, with help from the magazine's extremely capable garden staff. Throughout them all, the inimitable Bender style of writing will have you chuckling at unexpected moments. There's nothing dry or too technical in the pages of these three books.

The *Southern Living Garden Book* (Oxmoor House, 1998) is an A through Z guide to gardening in the South. Want to know what soil mix to use in your containers, how to build a simple compost pile, or how to root cuttings of special plants? It's all here, along with a long dictionary of plants for any situation, many illustrated with color photographs. If Steve Bender is writing, it's always fun reading.

The *Southern Living Garden Problem Solver* (Oxmoor House, 1999) is a perfect companion to the *Garden Book*. Many pictures and descriptions help you identify and treat a weak or diseased plant before things gets out of hand. Some of the pictures of bugs and insects in this book are so scary that I wouldn't suggest it for bedtime reading.

How to landscape a yard? That question intimidates homeowners, even those who have survived wading through hundreds of wallpaper and paint samples. Well, don't despair. Help is here in the form of the *Southern Living Landscape Book* (Oxmoor House, 2000). This book is helpfully divided into practical sections: Gardens of the South (40 of them), Planning Your Garden, Designing with Structures, Designing with Plants, Finishing Touches, Materials and Techniques, and Garden Makeovers.

For inspiration, I always turn to the books of the late Elizabeth Lawrence, landscape architect and plant lover extraordinaire. With charm, wit, and knowledge, she wrote about her two gardens, one in Charlotte and one in Raleigh. She described the plants advertised in farmers' market bulletins across the South, and the gardeners offering them for sale. Many letters and personal anecdotes make her books come to life and easy to read. There is also a scientific side to her writing, such as the long lists of blooming times for plants. She would go to great lengths to find out as much as she could about her plants, often sending samples to, and/or writing to, her many expert friends in the world of botany or horticulture. The first of her six books, *A Southern Garden: A Handbook for the Middle South* (UNC Press, 1942) recounts her experiences making a garden in Charlotte. We meet her gardening friends as well as her favorite plants. This book should be on every gardener's bookshelf.

Jim Wilson has written so many good gardening books for the South, and I highly recommend them all. One of his best books is called *Bulletproof Flowers for the South* (Taylor, Nov. 1999). This one is definitely on my Christmas list. My thoughtful friends Fran and Walter Bull gave me a copy of his invaluable reference book, *The South Carolina Gardener's Guide* (Cool Springs Press, 1997).

For general reference, I usually turn to *The American Hor-*

ticultural Society A-Z Encyclopedia of Garden Plants (DK Publishing, 1997). If you can't find what you need to know in this weighty tome with its 15,000 plants and 6,000 photographs, it's probably not worth knowing.

A book that will have you "hooting and hollering," according to garden writer Allen Lacy, is *Passalong Plants* (UNC Press, 1993). Written by that inimitable pair, Steve Bender and Felder Rushing, it will teach you about many old-fashioned plants that have been passed along among Southern gardeners for generations. As many of the plants are not available for sale, the book explains how to collect the seeds or take cuttings to root.

But there are more, so many more. I hate to leave any of my favorites out, so I have included a list of important gardening books in the bibliography

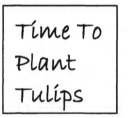

Time To Plant Tulips

There I was, the day after Christmas, on my hands and knees in the garden. Mounds of wrapping paper and a new book beckoned from indoors, but this was tulip-planting day. I had just retrieved my tulip bulbs from my parents' extra refrigerator (my old spare in our basement is on the fritz), where they had been spending an artificial winter.

I'll admit that it isn't too inviting to work outside in the cold weather, but there will be many mild days, so be ready.

Tulips planted too early will begin to sprout in our still-warm soil. Many Southern gardeners keep them in the refrigerator until planting time, from mid-November to mid-December in South Carolina's Upstate and from December to mid-January in its Midlands. If you don't have refrigerator room, keep them in the coolest place possible, such as an unheated garage or basement. Just don't allow them to freeze. You might try asking the supplier to ship your bulbs as late as possible, too. Tulips, and possibly hyacinths, are the only bulbs that get this treatment. Daffodils, crocuses, scillas, and most other spring bloomers are planted in fall because they are perennial. Tulips are essentially annuals for us. After they bloom, I pull them up and compost them, replacing them with summer annuals.

Sound like too much work for a short show? Maybe, but I can't imagine spring without a display of tulips. For the price you pay for a large cut flower arrangement, you can have beautiful color in your garden for up to three weeks. Plant them about six inches deep in well-prepared soil. I put mine in flower beds or containers, so it's easy. They don't need to be fertilized like perennial bulbs because everything they need to bloom was made inside the bulb last spring in Holland.

Although I try a few new ones each year, I've found some favorites. Tulips from the Darwin hybrid group do best for us, but I have had luck with a few tulips from the triumph hybrid group as well as the late-blooming lily-flowered type.

My all time favorite tulip is 'Elizabeth Arden', with a color that can only be described as frosted-lipstick pink with the tiniest hint of orange. It's very showy in the landscape, but I especially like it in large planters with deep-blue pansies. I use a soft yellow triumph group tulip called 'Yellow Present' in my window boxes tucked under the permanent planting of variegated ivy, because it is shorter and more in scale than some of the taller Darwin hybrids. Other favorites include white 'Ivory Floradale' and deep pink 'Queen of Bartigons',which seems to last a very long time in bloom.

The latest blooming tulips are the lily-flowered ones, and 'White Triumphator' is unequaled for a good show in the garden. For years, I've been trying to find a tulip that blooms

Tulips

late enough to complement a long border of Spanish bluebells (*Hyacinthoides hispanica*). The closest I've come so far is 'Daydream'. It boasts a luscious, apricot color that's suffused with orange. The bluebells still bloomed a bit later than the tulips, but the two did have a nice period where they coincided. This year I'm trying an even later blooming tulip called 'Dillenberg', an old variety described as "burnt orange/terra cotta and very fragrant."

One new combination for me this year is the tall yellow 'Mrs. Scheepers', another old favorite late tulip, planted behind an almost black-purple 'Queen of Night' tulip. The idea is that the dark flowers will shine in front of the lighter ones.

It's fun to experiment with some of the novelty varieties. I usually put these in containers. One that I love is 'New Design', a pink one with green-and-white variegated foliage. Actually, containers offer a way to get a big bang for your buck. Pick a prominent spot, such as either side of an entrance, and set out planters filled with colorful tulips, pansies, and alyssum, and wait for the compliments.

Five or six bulbs crammed into an eight-inch terra cotta pot, or a dozen or more planted in a whiskey barrel with pansies underneath, make a great display. You can plant a lot of small pots with one variety each, and then place them where they will make a splash. I've learned not to skimp when planting tulips in the landscape. Don't think in terms of a dozen, but plant at least twenty-five together and often a hundred or more in a flower bed.

When your tulips bloom, look around and see what else is blooming. Take notes for good combinations for the next year. In my garden, the Reeves spirea, lily-flowered tulips, Spanish bluebells, and mini 'Hawera' narcissuses all bloom together. My notes help me to know where to plant my tulips for next spring. Next fall, when I make my bulb order, I will know what areas will show the tulips to best advantage.

If you missed out on tulips this year, make a note on your calendar in early September to check out local garden centers, or send an order to one of the specialty suppliers. There may even be a few bulbs left at your garden center that you can still plant this year. I'd hate for you to miss out.

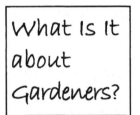

What Is It about Gardeners?

An Open Letter to my Future Grandchildren and Future Gardeners:

You'll have many friends during your life. The deepest, and longest-lasting friendships will be those with people with whom you have common values and interests.

Gardening offers numerous rewards. One easily overlooked is the opportunity to make friends with other gardeners. But if you're like me, you'll come to think of them more as soul sisters and brothers than friends. My gardening buddies and I are on the same wavelength. There's an understanding between us.

What is it about gardeners?

Gardeners are generous. They like to share their plants and their gardening experiences. Just ask one. They're eager participants in seed exchanges and plant swaps, and are always willing to cut off a branch from a favorite plant so you can root one for yourself.

Gardeners are optimistic. Who else would spend time and money, year after year, doggedly trying to transform our

Southern-fried backyards into cool, misty, English gardens?

Gardeners are inquisitive. Otherwise, how can you explain the huge market for gardening magazines, books, and videotapes. Television even has a Home and Garden cable channel. The more gardeners learn, the more they seem to want to know.

When I was about twelve years old, my granny and I would study the pictures and descriptions of woodland wild flowers in her field guide. Then we would look for them in the woods on our Chester County farm. After we dug them up, we'd plant them in my very first garden, in the shade of two old red cedar trees behind our farmhouse. I got to know all the plants by name. To this day, there are wild violets from that bed that escaped into the backyard and still bloom in the very early spring.

Gardeners are sociable. They enjoy each other's company, yet savor moments of solitude while tending their garden. They're joiners. They attend garden club meetings, belong to plant societies, and frequent gardening conferences.

Gardeners are artistic. It's not surprising that some gardeners, like Claude Monet, are painters, or aspire to be. The painter mixes colors on a canvas; the gardener mixes them in a garden. Gardening is a wonderful outlet for our need for creative expression. Are gardeners endowed with heightened sensory perceptions, or do they develop them through close contact with gardens of myriad colors, textures, tastes, and odors?

I can conjure up from childhood the smell of the rich, humusy, damp, black earth found on the shady bank of the creek on our farm. My Columbia garden is shady, so I can only dream about growing tomatoes, corn, and sunflowers — and what it would be like to garden in the sunshine. But for a little girl who grew up building log cabins in the woods, and walking barefoot down the middle of the creek, I'm not sure dirt would smell the same in the sun.

Gardeners are not tidy perfectionists. They can't help but get sweaty and dirty, and those meticulously manicured gardens in *Southern Living* magazine are literally snapshots of landscapes in motion. Turn your head, and a weed has popped up. Blink, and that neat bed has become overgrown. Knowing that gardens never achieve perfection, gardeners don't expect it in people either. Gardeners are very forgiving.

Thinking of my gardening buddies convinces me that Goethe must have had his fellow gardeners in mind when he wrote "To know someone, here or there, with whom you have understanding, in spite of distances, or thoughts unexpressed — that can make of this earth a garden."

May you be so blessed.

Love,
Orene

Bibliography

Armitage, Allan M. *Herbaceous Perennial Plants: A Treatise on their Identification, Culture, and Garden Attributes.* Athens, Ga.: Varsity Press, 1989.

Bender, Steve and Felder Rushing. *Passalong Plants.* Chapel Hill: University of North Carolina Press, 1993.

Bender, Steve, ed. *Southern Living Garden Book.* Birmingham: Oxmoor House, 1998.

—, ed. *Southern Living Garden Problem Solver.* Birmingham: Oxmoor House, 1999.

—, ed. *Southern Living Landscape Book.* Birmingham: Oxmoor House, 2000.

Bir, Richard E. *Growing and Propagating Showy Native Woody Plants.* Chapel Hill: University of North Carolina Press, 1992.

Brickell, Christopher and Judith D. Zuk, eds. *The American Horticultural Society A-Z Encyclopedia of Garden Plants.* New York: DK Publishing, 1997.

Campbell, Stu. *Let It Rot: The Gardener's Guide to Composting.* 3rd ed. Pownal, Vt.: Storey Communications, 1998.

Chaplin, Lois Trigg. *The Southern Gardener's Book of Lists: The Best Plants for All Your Needs, Wants, and Whims.* Dallas: Taylor Publishing, 1994.

Creasy, Rosalind. *The Complete Book of Edible Landscaping.* San Francisco: Sierra Club Books, 1982.

Dirr, Michael A. *Manual of Woody Landscape Plants: Their Identification, Ornamental Characteristics, Culture, Propagation and Uses.* 5th ed. Champaign, Ill.: Stipes Publishing, 1998.

Druse, Ken. *The Natural Garden*. New York: Clarkson Potter, 1989.

—, The *Natural Habitat Garden*. New York: Clarkson Potter, 1994.

—, The *Natural Shade Garden*. New York: Clarkson Potter, 1992.

Fletcher, June, Sarah Collins and Cynthia Crosson. "The Lazy Gardener." *Wall Street Journal*, 8 June 2001, Southeastern Edition: W1.

Glattstein, Judy, ed. "Gardener's World of Bulbs." *Brooklyn Botanic Garden Record Handbook* 127 (1991) Vol. 47, No. 2.

Harper, Pamela J. *Color Echoes: Harmonizing Color in the Garden*. New York: Macmillan, 1994.

Hart, Rhonda Massingham. *Deer-Proofing Your Yard & Garden*. Pownal, Vt.: Storey Communications, 1997.

Heath, Brent and Becky Heath. *Daffodils for American Gardens*. Washington: Elliott & Clark, 1995.

Huxley, Anthony, ed. *The New Royal Horticultural Society Dictionary of Gardening*. 4 vols. New York: Stockton Press, 1997.

Jekyll, Gertrude and Edward Mawley. *Roses for English Gardens*. 1902. Rpt. as *Roses*. Salem, N.H.: Ayer, 1983.

Kissam, J. B., ed. *1986 Agricultural Chemicals Handbook South Carolina*. Clemson University Cooperative Extension Service, Clemson, SC: 1986.

Lawrence, Elizabeth. *A Southern Garden: A Handbook for the Middle South*. Chapel Hill: University of North Carolina Press, 1942.

—. *The Little Bulbs: A Tale of Two Gardens*. New York: Criterion Books, 1957. Durham: Duke University Press, 1986.

Mickel, John T. *Ferns for American Gardens*. New York:

Macmillan, 1994.

Ogden, Scott. *Garden Bulbs for the South*. Dallas: Taylor, 1994.

Ottesen, Carole. *Ornamental Grasses: The Amber Wave*. New York: McGraw-Hill, 1989.

Reinhardt, Thomas A., Martina Reinhardt and Mark Moskowitz. *Ornamental Grass Gardening: Design Ideas, Functions and Effects*. Los Angeles: HP Books, 1989.

Scott, George Harmon. *Bulbs: How to Select, Grow and Enjoy*. Los Angeles: HP Books, 1982.

Shaw, Eva. *Shovel It: Nature's Health Plan*. Carlsbad, Calif.: Writeriffic, 2001.

Sheets, Kathy. "Oh, Deer!" *South Carolina Wildlife* March-April 1997: 34.

Verey, Rosemary. *The Garden in Winter*. New York: New York Graphic Society, 1988.

Wilson, Jim. *Bulletproof Flowers for the South*. Dallas: Taylor Publishing, 1999.

—. *Landscaping with Container Plants*. Boston: Houghton Mifflin, 1990.

—. *The South Carolina Gardener's Guide*. Franklin, Tenn.: Cool Springs Press, 1997.

Index